ROUTLEDGE LIBRARY EDITIONS:
ISLAM, STATE AND SOCIETY

Volume 7

ISLAM AND THE STATE

ISLAM AND THE STATE

P.J. VATIKIOTIS

LONDON AND NEW YORK

First published in 1987 by Croom Helm Ltd

This edition first published in 2017
by Routledge
2 Park Square, Milton Park, Abingdon, Oxon OX14 4RN

and by Routledge
711 Third Avenue, New York, NY 10017

Routledge is an imprint of the Taylor & Francis Group, an informa business

British Library Cataloguing in Publication Data
A catalogue record for this book is available from the British Library

ISBN: 978-1-138-23270-9 (Set)
ISBN: 978-1-315-31161-6 (Set) (ebk)
ISBN: 978-1-138-21982-3 (Volume 7) (hbk)
ISBN: 978-1-138-21984-7 (Volume 7) (pbk)
ISBN: 978-1-315-41445-4 (Volume 7) (ebk)

Publisher's Note
The publisher has gone to great lengths to ensure the quality of this reprint but points out that some imperfections in the original copies may be apparent.

Disclaimer
The publisher has made every effort to trace copyright holders and would welcome correspondence from those they have been unable to trace.

ISLAM AND THE STATE

P.J. VATIKIOTIS

CROOM HELM
London • New York • Sydney

Croom Helm Ltd, Provident House,
Burrell Row, Beckenham, Kent BR3 1AT

Croom Helm Australia, 44–50 Waterloo Road,
North Ryde, 2113, New South Wales

Published in the USA by
Croom Helm
in association with Methuen, Inc.
29 West 35th Street
New York, NY 10001

British Library Cataloguing in Publication Data

Vatikiotis, P.J.
Islam and the state.
1. Islam and politics
I. Title
297'.1977 BP173.7

ISBN 0–7099–2610–3

Library of Congress Cataloging-in-Publication Data

ISBN 0–7099–2610–3

Printed and bound in Great Britain
by Billings & Sons Limited, Worcester.

Contents

Introduction

When Indiana University invited me to give the Patten Foundation Lectures[1] in 1982/3, the committee responsible for this distinguished annual series in the humanities also suggested that I address myself in my lectures to the theme of Islam and the Nation-State. In accepting this kind invitation I was conscious of a delicate undertaking. Not only was Islam at that time a widely discussed subject among academics, but the activities and policies of Muslim states and unofficial popular Islamic organizations attracted world attention — and concern. My first responsibility then was to academic standards: to discuss a complex and 'explosive' subject with sense, candour and goodwill without allowing the discussion to degenerate into cheap polemic or facile sensationalism. To say too much could well demolish my non-specialist audience and generate more heat than light. To dismiss the subject in a very captious treatment was to risk offending both my audience and my Muslim colleagues and friends. I settled on a concise introduction of the most salient features of a potential full treatment of the subject from an historical, doctrinal-legal and existential perspective. The lectures delivered on the Patten Foundation are reproduced here in Chapters 2 and 3.[2]

Over 20 years ago, E.I. Rosenthal published his *Islam and the National State*.[3] However, the two major attempts by Western scholars this century to examine Islam in the modern world were those by W.C. Smith, *Islam in Modern History*,[4] and H.A.R. Gibb, *Modern Trends in Islam*.[5] Earlier, the latter had edited a co-authored volume which considered the various aspects of the relation between Islam and modernity. Published by the Oxford University Press in 1931 as *Whither Islam?*, the chapter by Kamppfmeyer on the Society of Muslim Brothers in Egypt constituted at that time a singular, original contribution. Gibb's introduction and conclusion to the volume were thought-provoking pieces. Essentially a scholar of Arabic literature, Gibb concentrated his research on the impact of the 'modern world' on the literary, cultural and political response of Islam and Muslims. Himself the product of a missionary upbringing, Gibb sought desperately to explore the possibilities of a modern *ethic* in Islam for Muslims. In doing so he may on occasion have tended to misinterpret the nature of Islam as an historical religious movement. Nevertheless, his seminal work, *Modern Trends*, set the boundaries if not parameters of the discussion of the relation of Islam to the modern world.

The efforts of these scholars had been preceded by those of the American orientalist in Egypt, C.C. Adams, whose *Islam and Modernism in Egypt* was published by the Oxford University Press in 1933. It was basically a biography of Sheikh Muhammad Abduh (d.1905), the most illustrious — though not necessarily most successful — Egyptian Islamic modernist of the late nineteenth and early twentieth centuries. There was also the work of another great Islamic modernist and reformer, Mohammad Iqbal in India.[6] Indeed, much of the debate about the role of Islam in state and society took place in two major centres of the Muslim world — Egypt and the Indian sub-continent. By and large, it still does, particularly if we consider the writings of Sayyid Qutb and his disciples in the former and those of Abu al-Ala' al-Mawdudi, Abu al-Hasan al-Nadví and their disciples in the latter.

There were also the more popular writings of journalists, travellers and publicists on the revival of Islam, the reaction of Muslims to the concatenation of world events from the turn of the century to the end of the Great War, dominated as these events were by Christian European powers; and developments in the relations between Europeans and Islam, or more specifically, European powers and new — as well as older — Muslim states, going as far back as the Napoleonic conquest of Egypt in 1798, the French conquest of Algeria in 1830, the British occupation of Egypt in 1882, British involvement in Persia from the 1890s to the 1920s, relations with the ailing Ottoman state from the 1830s to the end of the Great War, and the more romantic, albeit bloody, episode of the Mahdist state in the Sudan (1880s–1890s). Thus, for example, the American journalist, Philip Stoddard's *The World of Islam*, first published in 1920, is the model for much more recent publications in the latest spate of European-Western concern with political Islam, such as John Laffin, *The Dagger of Islam*, or a number of volumes on the resurgence of Islam.[7]

One could argue that by the 1930s enough of the published work of Islamic modernists/reformers had become available to Western scholars for them — that is, Gibb and others — to react to the whole Islamic reformist movement by trying to assess its strengths and weaknesses, as well as understand its problems and evaluate its prospects.

The inter-war period, however, was dominated in Muslim lands by the political ascendancy of secularist governing elites promoting a secular political ideology, nationalism. Their special relationship with European powers, with Britain foremost among the latter, tended to encourage and strengthen their promotion of local nationalism and the establishment of secular national political institutions. In fact, one could argue that this relationship also acted as a constraint on these elites against their reversion to the more traditional, i.e. religious, overtone or ethos in their political life. One notes that this reversion was made easier upon the retreat of European power from the lands of Islam, and the severance of the link between it and Muslim governing elites, a process that began as early as the 1930s.

May I remind my reader once again that what is presented here relates to an interpretation of the relation between religion and politics in Islam in general, and its relation to the state and the nation-state in particular. The content and approach are not based on a strictly theoretical examination of ideas in Islam, but on the relation of these ideas to political events — to the historical experience of Muslim society, and the evolution of Islamic belief and practice in the crucible of actual experience. To this extent the original lectures and corollary essays are united by a uniform approach. Their diversity, on the other hand, illustrates my contention that the perennial problematic confusion among Muslims regarding the relation between religion and their political order(s) is too complex to be dealt with by facile generalization; more importantly, that revealed or not, religious belief and the Sacred Law are also very much what men living in society and buffeted by events in time and space, make of them, as much as the belief and law themselves in turn influence the behaviour of these same men and their understanding of their world. One could not otherwise explain the differences between, say, Islam in Egypt and the Fertile Crescent — practised by basically settled peasant and urban communities — and Islam in the Arabian Peninsula, the North African desert, Black Africa, or insular Southeast Asia.

Although originally in the Patten Lectures this work began with a preliminary and cursory consideration of Islam and the nation-state, as a result of parallel work it expanded to encompass the wider concern about Islam and politics. After the Distinguished Visiting Professor Lectures I delivered at the American University in Cairo in April 1986 on the broad theme, 'Reason and Passion in Politics', and based exclusively on the record of Western European political thought and experience from classical Greek times to the so-called post-industrial or high technology age, I became convinced that my having moved on from the initial narrow issue of Islam and the nation-state to the wider theme of Islam and politics was inevitable and arguably salutary. My private debate with the Egyptian writer Husein Ahmad Amin, occasioned by his two major works, *Dalil al-muslim al-hazin* and *Hawla al-daŵa ila tatbiq al-sharīʿa* (Beirut, 1983 and 1984 respectively) further confirmed for me the need to treat the wider theme.[8]

Current events themselves, ranging from the unending Gulf war between two Muslim states, Iran and Iraq, in a dispute over territory — a central feature of the nation-state and only one of several conflicts in the community of believers — and at the same time the demand of Muslims in the Spanish zone of Morocco for representation based on religious identity in an environment of long-standing nationalist assertion; or the separatist demands of Muslim communities in the states of the Philippines, Thailand and elsewhere in the Far East, all of them movements that are in direct opposition to and a negation of the concept of the nation-state, further complicate the whole question of Islam and politics, adding to the weight of its dialectic and rendering it an urgent topic for examination.

When one of our current research students, a tribesman by origin and now a young captain in the religious corps of the Royal Jordanian Army, frequently reminds us that the new generation of his compatriots and more widely in his part of the world is more attached to the Islamic religious tradition and that he, himself, in recognition of this situation, is researching the relevance of Koranic exegesis to the resolution of the problems of contemporary society, the topicality of the unresolved relation between Islam and politics is further highlighted. When another of our Muslim research students with great enthusiasm coupled simultaneously with tremendous anxiety and apprehension, inquires into the deliberately lost or wasted role of women in the development of contemporary Saudi society, the central importance of the nexus Islam and politics to the life and future evolution of Muslim societies is placed into striking focus.

A particular question about the Islamic world has always concerned me ever since I left that world to come to the Anglo-Saxon one of Britain and the United States. It has remained with me not primarily because of my academic pursuits in the university of teaching and writing about that world, but more as a result of prolonged direct involvement with and experience of life as a child and youth in that world and society. The question is this: Whatever else it may or may not do, can an Islamic political order create a new society, one that is basically 'middle class' with common or shared values, a common attitude or mind, even its own morality, and one that can cope reasonably with the problems — the demands, contradictions and discontents — of modernity? For, with historical hindsight it may be asserted that religious faith (any religious faith) is both the foundation of society and the rock on which it can be shipwrecked, and the nation perish . . .

Where in Chapters 6 and 7 I point to serious differences (with practical political consequences) between the experience of Islam and that of Europe, I must inform my reader that these differences are not simply extrapolated or inferred from texts of Islamic history, theology or law. They are in fact empirically observed in recurrent occasions of actual meetings and debates between us and Muslim colleagues, when dealing with real, often mundane, issues of political, economic and social importance and practicality.

I happen to believe that before two rather different societies can together seek ways of cooperation and mutual understanding, they should be quite clear about what separates them. If this were not the case in the first place, they would not proceed to seek ways of getting closer to one another. A great deal of mindless talk goes on in conventions, conferences, college common rooms and the media about these matters.

Primarily, though, I was moved to elaborate on the original three Patten Lectures as a result of my long discussions with Ambassador Husein Ahmad Amin of Egypt in 1978–86, and the impact of his writings about his own Muslim society. One of our more prolonged exchanges was occasioned by my reaction to a section in his best-selling book, *Dalil al-muslim al-hazin* (1983) where, after a brilliant exposition using stringent historical criticism of the Abu Lahab episode with the Prophet Mohammad, he ends up with the attractive traditional invocation, 'and God after all this knows best what He intended'. I called my friend to task: how could he claim a critical historical method when at the end he invokes God's knowledge of the unknown? 'Ah', he said, 'this is a perfectly "scientific" ending to the discussion.' He threw my tentative definition or characterization of secularism of a few days earlier in the lecture hall of the Egyptian Diplomatic Institute back into my face. 'Remember', he said, 'there is no finality, etc.'

Equally stimulating over the years had been my periodic discussions (whenever I visited Cairo) with the two leading secularists in Egypt, Dr Louis Awad (a Christian) and Maître Tawfiq al-Hakim (a Muslim). Two other prominent secularists influenced my consideration of this theme in a different way: Dr Boutros Boutros Ghali, one-time Professor of Political Science at Cairo University and, since October 1977, Minister of State for Foreign Affairs, and Professor Magdi Wahba, Emeritus Professor of English and English Literature at Cairo University and one-time under-secretary in the Ministry of Culture. Although both of them are confirmed secularists of long standing in education, life-style and professional conduct, they nevertheless attach great value and allow a central role to their communal — in this case, Coptic — identity and community. Their secularism, that is to say, does not go so far as to permit the replacement of this identity and community by a wider integrated one, and especially not an Arab-Islamic one. Of the younger generation, the historian Tariq el-Bishri represented for me the live experience of a historian trying to steer a reasonable course between the demands of modern, secular historical scholarship and the less tangible but none the less powerful constraints of a religious and cultural anchor in the Islamic tradition.[9] Other members of Bishri's generation, my friends Aliy Hillal Dessouki and Saadedin Ibrahim, managed to find a relatively comfortable — if not intellectual at least academic — 'home' in the presumed ethical–ideological neutrality of modern American-style academic social science. Another of our mutual friends, the engaging and constantly fretting Ibrahim Saqr and the historians Raouf Abbasaur and Abdel Azim Ramadan never shared this comfortable feeling. Many others managed to escape for a time at least the debilitating and conscience-binding constraints of the Islamic nexus by embracing the least realistic of the secular approaches (least realistic for their consensus), that of Western Marxism. And yet, I was even more determined to carry on with the examination of the issue here as a result of my close association with colleagues and friends of the last school. In witnessing the gaping chasm between their verbal formulations, their exchanges in polite discussion and their personal and social behaviour and values, I only gasped at their anachronistic thought. They bordered on the dinosauric, if not the fossilized. Their social thought, or what they attempted to express as social thought, was primarily of archaeological interest. Yet I realize and appreciate the risk involved: to abandon their rigid anachronistic position is to betray their very lives and selves.

The consideration of Islam and the nation-state is occasioned by the relation and connection of the recent rise of independent states in the Islamic world to modern European history and the experience of two world wars within the space of half a century — as well as to the crucial position and role of these states in a global East-West ideological political conflict — to that extent it is one that should be of wider concern and interest. But my decision to embark on this discussion was also prompted by my own personal experience of life in Muslim societies, as well as my personal links with members of those societies, students, colleagues and friends with and around whom I grew up.

I have always viewed Islam in political terms. To some extent this view may have been greatly influenced by my work 35 years ago on the Ismaili-Fatimid movement in the ninth to eleventh centuries AD.[10] But it was also immediately affected by my personal youthful experience of the Arab-Jewish conflict in Palestine in the period from 1936 to 1947, as well as my subsequent immediate experience of the rising wave of Muslim Brotherhood violent political activity while an undergraduate in Egypt in the period 1944–8. Close personal relations of long standing with individual Muslims — schoolmates, or fellow undergraduates, their homes and families — as well as with groups, clubs and organizations, further nurtured this political-cultural view of Islam. I came to view it as more than a religion; as a whole tradition and a political culture.

This is one reason why my interest in political or militant Islam of the last 20 years is very much linked to the political order. If the latter has been dominated for a long time by the nation-state — its most common component unit of political structure/organization — can the nation-state system fulfil the religio-political demands of Islam? The question became real in my mind when I observed the persistent contradictions in the political behaviour of Muslims within the nation-state, outside and beyond it. It became even more important and relevant for the 'world order' if such in fact exists. Does Islam, quiescent, pacific, militant or otherwise, constitute an international political movement with definite goals that can and have been articulated? Or is Islam a handy device by which weak states (among which happen to be many Islamic ones) try to make demands on the more powerful ones?

Assuming there is an international political movement — even a revolutionary one — which we call Islam or Islamic resurgence, are its goals capable of political solution by anyone, or are they primarily emotive and symbolic and therefore unsatisfiable and never-ending?

Is the current phenomenon of the militant Islamic movement a pressing one? Have there been previous periods of militant Islamic international pressure and action? What causes such a movement? How did the state system cope with it in the past, both at the level of the domestic nation-state as well as of the international order of nation-states? Is the movement now a threat to both the established nation-state regimes and the international order of nation-states?

In this study we look, in passing, at the extent to which existing nation-states cope with the Islamic religio-political movement on the national level. We do not, however, more than allude to the extent to which the structures of the present world order cope with such a movement that proclaims that it spurns international custom, law and practice. Therefore, we do not consider the important matter of how far or well the present world order of nation-states can allow conflicting religious-cultural values to play a role in international politics and relations between nation-states. Do peace and world order depend on the elimination of value conflicts and not merely on interest and power differences? If such peace and order also depend on the principle of non-interference in the internal affairs of a nation-state, how illegal or illegitimate is an Islamic international movement for which such interference and hegemony are essential requirements?

If this, in very abbreviated form, is a plausible albeit captious formulation of the relations between Islam and the nation-state, what are the prospects, if any, of secular politics in Islamic lands? On the whole, clearly not too bright. On the other hand, one cannot cavalierly overlook or ignore the long-standing reality of secular administrations in several territorially defined and internationally recognized sovereign states, the societies or populations of which are overwhelmingly Muslim. Furthermore, the political life of some 100 million Arab Muslims for the past 80 years has been conducted in such independent nation-states: Egypt, Iraq, Syria, Lebanon, Jordan, etc. Litigation, civil, commercial and criminal disputes between them have been regulated by man-made laws in secular, national courts of law. Officially the constitutional basis of their political system and sovereign legal authority has rested on the legitimacy notion of popular sovereignty, the myth common in the Western nation-state that legitimacy derives from the consensus of a political community in which sovereignty belongs to the people — its members or citizens. This is clearly contrary to the Islamic insistence that sovereignty belongs to God and that the legitimacy of earthly authority in the state rests on the implementation of the sovereign God's will and Sacred Law. One can easily refer to direct statements by Muslim writers denying the notion of popular sovereignty as the basis of legitimate authority in an Islamic state, and counter them with statements by other Muslim writers insisting on the popular limitation and accountability of power in the Islamic state.

What one is really faced with is an existential reality of several secularly-administered territorial nation-states in the world of Islam at one level, and an idealized model on a higher level, which one may refer to as the myth of the Islamic state, religiously based and defined, ultimately governed by God and/or His revealed Sacred Law. The dichotomy has been with us for nearly 1,500 years and is likely to persist, giving rise on the way to periodic demands by Muslims for the realization of the Islamic political ideal by the rejection or overthrow of the temporal or mundane reality. It is most unlikely that the attendant problems of this dichotomy will disappear completely — viz., those of integrated plural nation-states, secular conceptions of citizenship, not based on religious identity or status. One may expect a prolonged period of nation-states, members of the comity of nations, whose populations are Muslim, but not always their governments in the strictest sense of the term.

In view of the nuclear threat, diminishing world resources, the advance and proliferation of infectious or otherwise transmitted and epidemic diseases, famines and civil wars, will adherence to Islam remain as strong or become more tenacious, or will it be abandoned altogether? Will the so-called North–South contest end up as one between Afro-Asian Islam and European-Western Christendom with the Mediterranean basin acting as a bridge or moat between them?[11]

But are the prospects of the nation-state in Europe — its home base — all that bright? Will the nation-state evolve into a new structure or a totally different one, or might it disappear altogether? Its recent record has not been all that brilliant.[12] Given Islam's rejection of the nation-state and European dissatisfaction with its recent behaviour, might we witness a reversion to the broader political arrangements of an earlier historical period or some variation thereof?[13]

It is not so much that Islam makes no provision for a nation-state. For that matter neither does any other monotheistic religion. Rather it is a question of a different conception of the nation-state. Some Muslims in fact argue with great conviction that the state made its first appearance with Islam, for Islam was first embodied in a state (Medina) and a nation (the Arab tribes around Yathrib). It arose as a state and a nation. The Islamic state was now (632 AD) there in order to proclaim the message of Islam, the Islamic faith, on a universal scale.[14] Thus, Islam has been the only monotheistic religious movement of supra-national, universal human scope. To this extent, Islam rejects common national barriers, based on territorial frontiers, and ethnic-linguistic and racial differences. The latter are, after all, relative features or phenomena. As a strictly unitarian religion, or creed, Islam rejects these mundane specificities so peculiar to the 'religion of Abraham'. Unlike earlier religions, Islam did not stop at the call to the faith. It proceeded to the establishment of a state which embodied a new nation, that of the believers, or the faithful: *ummat al-mu'*minin. The very basis of this new nation and its nationalism, if you wish, has been the religion of Islam. The state has been and remains its instrument. The state, therefore, has no value in itself; nor is it set up temporally for a particular people, as a nation-state, to the exclusion of others. Rather, it is based on the universal principle of Islam to safeguard the religion and extend its message. Islam, in other words, is integrative or has integrative ambitions on a universal scale.[15]

Nationalism (*qawmiyya*) as an ideology is incompatible with the world of Islam, for it implies a pre-Islamic kind of tribal particularism, *jahiliyya*. In fact, nationalism is Islam's greatest (deadliest?) enemy, for it represents an attempt to separate Islam from politics and isolate it from the resolution of temporal matters. That is, it postulates the separation between religion and politics, religion and the state, or it denies Islam its central role in the regulation of Muslim earthly political affairs.

The nation state in Islam is then an ideological, not a territorial concept.[16] It comprises the community of the faithful or believers wherever they may be. The state, on the other hand, is the structure of temporal-secular power which protects the community, the nation or the *umma* against its external — infidel — enemies, and ensures that the believers can lead the life of observant Muslims. It guarantees, that is, the implementation and upholding of the Sacred Law, the *sharia*, by governing according to its precepts. In this sense, the contention that Islam is *din wa dawla*, religion and state, recognizes the sanctity of power. *Din* is not simply the faith or creed of Islam, but the totality of the believer's conduct — especially his public conduct — which renders him a good Muslim.

The territorial nation-state, based on nationality, and the relatively modern European concept of nationalism — which integrates a national community under a secular law of the land applied uniformly to all citizens regardless of religious belief — is rejected by Islamic doctrine. It is also opposed today by the several militant Islamic religious movements, generally referred to in this work as Radical Islam. The political community in this instance is coterminous with the community of believers. The insistence upon this congruence has generated several problems which this tract attempts to outline.

Yet one is impressed by the tenacity of the state institution in Islam as a structure of temporal, indeed secular, power. For several decades now, at least since 1920, the 'modern' secular state has been the legitimate foundation of political life, and at least official, group identity. As such, though, it has also contributed to the centrifugal tendencies in the *umma*, the Islamic Nation, so bitterly deplored and intensely abhorred by the new Muslim militants. But one is equally aware of the state's historical as well as continued separation from the nation, more precisely, from society. Widespread authoritarianism and autocracy in several Muslim countries in recent times may be in part the outcome of this separation, as well as its cause.

Adherents of Islamic movements insist that there can be no genuine Islamic state unless and until its rulers implement rigorously the Word and Law of God, thus enabling the believers to live complete, integrated Muslim lives. No believer can or must accept any law or regulation that derives from non-Muslim sources. The modern barbaric and infidel (*jahiliyya*) domination of man by man must give way to that of God over man. Nor can the believer accept a ruler — or state — who does not govern by the precepts of God's revealed law.

The question, then, is whether the modern state can integrate the nation either on the basis of man's law or that of God. So far it has done neither. For the Radical Muslim the question is also whether Islam can bring the state and society together again and join power to the Sacred Law; that is, bring it under its jurisdiction and control. However, if the Word of God triumphs in the rule over men and the only transcendent referrent for a Muslim political, or public, order is a divine one, one must consider the problems arising in connection with individual rights, the citizen versus the state, citizenship and the political integration of the other, that is, the non-Muslim.

In the meantime, the sharp ideologization of Islam by radical ideologues has made religion into a potent ideological force which challenges territorial rule in many states today. Historically, on the whole, religion-based identity has resisted the secular integration of nationalism, and politics itself in many Muslim countries has been understood and regarded as a variant of religion, if not religion incarnate. What Carleton Coon called the religious and ethnic mosaic of the Middle East[17] has tended to ignore — in certain cases, even reject — the national boundaries so recently imposed upon it. Movements of religious reform, imported ideas and institutions of nationalism and constitutionalism were used to reconcile the belief system, cultural perception and traditional institutions of an earlier age to the requirements of the modern Western state system without much success. Unfortunately, there was no philosophical commitment to secularism and its values of scepticism, experimentation and tolerance, so essential to pluralistic politics. With one or two exceptions, states have arisen in the Middle East which are not nation-states. As a political concept, the nation-state is characterized by authority that is territory-based, not by universalist, extra-territorial conceptions of it.

The term nation-state is, therefore, misleading when applied to the several countries in the Middle East, because in most of them the nation is considered in religious terms to encompass those beyond and across the territorial boundaries of the individual states. There is a constant clash between the exigencies of the modern territorial state, and the wider nation, or community of believers, which, until the recent past, was governed by reference to religious precepts, and to what was believed to be God's revealed pattern for the universe.

Caught between the burden of tradition — with its insistence upon the supremacy of the nation of Islam, the *umma* — and the requirements of the modern territorial secular nation-state, temporal governments in the Middle East found themselves set on a dangerous course. Lebanon and Iran, two recent examples, both foundered. Failing to construct regimes outside religion, one collapsed into chaos, the other succumbed to the tyranny of a near-medieval theocracy. In Lebanon, territorial gave way to sectarian jurisdiction and nationality. In Iran, the dominant Shii community of believers ignores territorial boundaries and seeks to extend its 'universal truth' among fellow-believers across boundaries. Such notions of power and authority based on religion and ideology suggest that in Muslim societies the legitimization of power is still widely contested and authority is tenuous.

More glaring has been the failure of the secularists — of the Right and the Left — in modern times to make secularism the accepted ideology of society. This way they might have gained the loyalty of the public to the nation-state and the allegiance of the majority of its members to its political order. Except for a time at the beginning of this century and during the inter-war period, secularists opted for supranational ideologies, such as pan-Arabism, turning their attention away from the concerns of the territorially defined individual nation-state. Their new concept of the nation-state was ethnically integrative across boundaries and near-imperial in its territorial limits or demarcation — the Arab nation being defined as comprising all Arabs wherever they may be found in the Middle East. At the same time, they failed to resolve the matter of the role of Islam in the nation-state, or in society under the new secular nation-state, and ignored the problems of citizenship based either on *jus solis* or *jus sanguinis*, but free of any religious, sectarian qualification. Thus they too, in turn, after the Muslim modernist reformers of the late nineteenth and early twentieth centuries, failed to integrate the community within an acceptable public order.[18]

The debate among Muslims over the role of the *sharia* in the state continues. In short, the question of religion and state remains open. Actually the *umma*, the community of believers, itself lacks consensus over major political issues; nation-states within the *umma* have broken ranks with the community of the faithful following their respective secularly perceived national-state interest. A recent example of this is the conclusion of a peace treaty in 1979 between Israel (for long proclaimed as the single greatest enemy of the Muslim community) and Egypt, home of al-Azhar and centre of the study of the religious sciences of Islam.

Iran and Iraq have been locked in a deadly war over a territorial dispute regarding the Gulf for the last six years at very great material and human cost. The war developed into a Sunni versus Shii sectarian conflict and into an Arab versus Persian ethnic one. It has given rise to other manifestations of disarray in the *umma*, especially in the ranks of the Arab states. Most important for our discussion is the fact that a self-proclaimed, militant Islamic regime in Tehran is fighting a typical war as a nation-state against another nation-state, Iraq. The Islamic rationalization for it is the objective of overthrowing a 'heretical, infidel, deviant, usurping, tyrannical regime' in Baghdad for the greater glory of Islam.

In the Introduction and Chapter One we look generally at the overall problem of religion and state in historical and analytical terms. Chapter Two deals more directly with Islam and the nation-state. Chapter Three is a discussion of the origins and features of recent radical or militant Islam, the demand for the return of Islam to politics, and its implications for the nation-state. Chapter Four surveys the problem of secularism by opposing Islam to nationalism. The hegemonist aspirations of political Islam are examined further in Chapter Five, which deals with non-Muslims in Muslim society.

If the above suggests a serious difference between the implications of Islam for political order and in this case that of the nation-state, setting it aside from the experience of the rest of the modern world or international system of nation-states, Chapter Six is intended to identify more clearly what separates the Islamic from the non-Islamic historical-political experience of Europe. The separation is further highlighted by the episode of the oil crisis between East and West, or Europe and the Islamic world, in the 1970s. It is also linked to the radical

Islamic or Muslim rejection of Western modernity. I raise, in passing, both general and specific questions about Islam and the nation-state on the domestic and international levels, partly on the basis of a brief reference to the relations between several Arab Muslim states as these were affected by recent events.

The difficult and largely unresolved problem of religion and state will recur periodically. What I have tried to do here with some trepidation is to define the problem and the parameters of its discussion from a non-Muslim perspective. However, no outsider can presume to resolve the problem; he can only participate occasionally in the debate about it.

I wish to thank the Patten Foundation and Indiana University for offering me a forum in which to discuss some of these matters, and for their kind and generous hospitality. Publication of this tract was postponed several times: other commitments, as well as a recent long spell of ill-health caused the delay.

In acknowledging the assistance over the years of several colleagues and friends in the slow gestation of this study, I wish to pay tribute to an old colleague and friend, the late Edward Buehrig. It was at his suggestion, as a member of the Patten Foundation Committee, that I initiated a discussion of the theme 'Islam and Politics' in the Patten Foundation Lectures. I must also express my appreciation to Ambassador Husein Ahmad Amin of Egypt for his stimulating discussions of several aspects of political Islam as well as his enlightening, charming and engaging correspondence in response to my comments on his published works; a truly erudite, thoughtful, considerate and generous friend and colleague. Several aspects of the problem discussed in these lectures and essays also reflect the sustained interest over the past 20 years of MSc and research students in classrooms and seminars, especially that part of the paper's syllabus dealing with tradition and politics. A succession of research students in the last ten years have, through their research and questioning, contributed further to this debate. Several have, during their supervision sessions, contributed a great deal to this debate. Needless to say, I alone am responsible for what is presented here.

No doubt there will be many discussions of political Islam in years to come. The most encouraging development so far is the prolific, varied and sustained debate conducted by Muslims among themselves. Interest by Western students must now move beyond the limited mundane concerns of national and international policy, to consider whether the study of this wave of Islamic activism — and assertiveness — by them will be qualitatively different and/or more or less enlightening than that of their predecessors' study of the Islamic reform movement earlier this century.

The attempts by the West earlier in this century to make over some part of the *umma*, politically at least, into its own image have not simply failed; they were finally rejected unequivocally by the Muslims themselves, who did not feel they were the beneficiaries or recipients of a beneficent arrangement, but the victims of a superimposed new and alien experiment in social and political organization. Their arguments for this rejection seem to boil down to the assertion that Muslims already have their own superior ideology, social and political values and perceptions; in short, they insist they are different, so different in fact that, in their view, Western ideologies and schemes for social and political arrangements are not inapplicable and inefficient because they are irrelevant to Islam and Muslim society only, but also because they are contrary to and inferior to the religion of Islam and its precepts. If this is the case, then one must consider more seriously the ideological and practical basis of this perceived difference, sense of superiority and excellence and already proclaimed and often repeated rejection.

There will be those who find my approach to a dialogue between non-Muslim and Muslim too direct and idiosyncratic. I feel I cannot preach to those who proclaim a vast cultural-ethical difference between their and my worlds; I can only argue with them. I cannot be like the European politician who exhorted his North African counterparts to develop their national economies in such a way as to promote ever greater exports. The puzzled North Africans retorted in a plaintive manner: Even when we do, your countries will not buy any of our exports, because your countries prefer protectionist trade policies. If I underline occasionally certain contradictions of attitude and/or behaviour on the part of my Muslim contemporaries and remind them uncomfortably of the less attractive aspects of their history, this is no more than the complaint of some Muslim writers themselves about the over-romanticization of the Islamic past, and their rejection of it. At least I am not un-solicitously insulting their intelligence by telling them how right they are in their quaintly narcissistic evaluation of their own superiority, unique importance to the world and God-given right to exclusive domination of it.[19] Instead I hope I remind them that they cannot ignore or stand aside from modernity; somehow they must confront it, and come to grips with its peculiar problems and challenges. If they believe their Islamic faith, tradition and culture can do this, they must also be aware of its capabilities and limitations, and of the fact that, so far, Islam has failed to cope adequately or satisfactorily with these problems; that it finds it difficult to accommodate certain dimensions of modernity; that it invariably resorts to a restorative stand: a return to the traditional idiom of the fathers and the reinstatement of traditional standards of morality without, however, the formulation of an acceptable relevant and applicable public ethic. Confrontation rather than cooperation has been, so far, Islam's chosen approach to the modern world. Rejection, rather than rapproachement or even accommodation, is its more recent preferred reaction to that world.

What we have tried to discuss here is the background, basis and reasons for these difficulties, and a reasonable assessment or evaluation of the prospects. And to borrow my friend Husein Amin's closing remark, at the risk of betraying my own secularist position, I conclude: 'And God after all this knows best what He intended'. Yet I adhere jealously to the admonition to the Greeks by Homer in the *Iliad* and Tyrtaeus in the *Elegy*: 'It is an extravagant indulgence to shift the responsibility for a public ethic and order on to the deity — God, Allah or whatever. It is at the same time arrogant to make extravagant claims for an ideology which purports to assist God to establish His writ over man's earthly state, in order to set the Muslim on earth above the rest of humanity.' Or, as the historian Barbara Tuchman, put it, 'God's interference does not acquit man of folly. Rather it is man's device for transferring responsibility for folly.'[20]

1

Islam and the State: A Historical Survey

It is useful to recapitulate briefly — even to encapsulate — the history of the civilization and lands we are dealing with when considering Islam and the nation-state.

The Arabs under the Umayyads created in less than one hundred years, from AD 660 to 750, the conditions in which a new Islamic civilization could be built in the great urban centres of the ancient Near East. Although the conception of the state was alien to them, since they were a tribal society which knew no citizens — only kinsmen united by blood ties — they nevertheless provided a stable centralized state to control their rapidly expanding empire, with an administration more elaborate than anything the Arabs had known before. It was this which allowed a conquering, politically and socially dominant minority of mainly Christian, pagan and Zoroastrian populations to consolidate Islam and quickly subjugate the Semitic and Iranian worlds.

By the time the Umayyad Caliphate in Damascus gave way to the Abbasid in Baghdad in 750, the Arab conquests had politically unified a large part of the world from Spain to India. The widespread use of a common language, Arabic (a new *lingua franca* for that area), facilitated the exchange of ideas. The fact that the central lands of the Nile and Tigris-Euphrates valleys that were conquered had had settled urban civilizations for millennia also helped. Then their immunity from external attack for nearly 400 years, from the middle of the seventh to the middle of the eleventh century, enabled the Islamic dominion to promote a vast free-trade area without barriers, permitting the development of commerce which, in turn, created a wealthy middle class of merchants, traders, bankers, craftsmen, artisans and professional men. Some of these, in turn, patronized learning and the arts, the development of which was also assisted by the use of paper, thus creating a rich, sophisticated society, so much admired by the rest of the world.

The Abbasids promoted further a cosmopolitan civilization with Baghdad as its centre and Arabic as its *lingua franca*. It was not specifically a Muslim one, since only its language, law and theology were that. The rest of its ingredients came from non-Muslim sources, such as Greek philosophy and science (which as we shall see were later rejected with significant consequences), and Persian and Indian influences. Its culture was multiracial, since much of its philosophical literature was written by Christians and Jews; its medical and mathematical treatises were written by Persians and Indians.

And yet two epochal developments — one fairly early, the other later — led to the collapse initially of the Arab and subsequently of the more cosmopolitan Muslim civilization. The first one was the break-up of the Caliphate, the disintegration of the political unity of the Islamic dominion. This was due in part to the restlessness and upheavals of the non-Arab converts, the rise of heresies and other religio-political movements among them, and the transformation of the military system by the introduction of that institution so unique to Islam, slave armies and praetorian garrisons, which rendered the Caliphate an otherwise powerless spiritual office. They inaugurated the Sultanate, a secular institution, based strictly on power. The weakness of the Caliphate allowed the usurpation of power by provincial governors and other satraps who founded short or long-lived dynasties at will. The break-up of the political unity of Islam was a reality by the middle of the eighth century when Abdel Rahman set up an independent state in Spain. By the beginning of the tenth century, a third rival Caliphate, the Fatimid in North Africa and Egypt, added to the disintegration.

Political events were not the only disrupters of the political unity of Islam. Religious, cultural and economic changes contributed to it too. Pre-Islamic religious influences in Iran led to theological dissension and revolutionary messianism. A revival of Persian local or parochial sentiment expressed itself in a proliferation of Manichean and millenarian sects. In the heart of Islam the battle raged for a time between those who were attracted by Greek rational philosophy on one side and, on the other, those insisting upon the pre-eminence of the revealed word of God as the only explanation of human and natural phenomena.

Despite all these challenges and political disruption, the Muslim world enjoyed, until the eleventh century, economic and other prosperity. The possession of a common language outweighed the loss of political unity. After that, however, the *Islamic realm* was subjected to a new threat, that of external attack from the desert and steppe nomads of Central Asia, culminating in the Mongol devastation 250 years later. City life decayed and, since medieval Islamic civilization was essentially urban and its material basis that of commercial wealth, economic prosperity declined. Islamic cities, however, had never developed self-governing institutions or defence arrangements like those of their contemporary Lombard and Hanseatic Leagues. Consequently, primary loyalty in them was not civic but religious, an important fact for our subject. Their inhabitants had no common civic loyalty; they were not genuine burghers. Muslims, Jews and Christians coexisted, but in separately designated quarters.

In the meantime, the destruction wreaked by external foes and senseless conquerors, and the loss of political unity were paralleled by the loss of linguistic and cultural unity, when the intellectual monopoly of the Arabic language was broken by the revival of Persian and later by Turkish. Thus, Arab philosophy was in effect dead by 1200 and Arab science two hundred years later. Christian Europe acquired through the Renaissance a secular tradition with its background of Greek rationalism and science. The only tradition behind Islam was the proclaimed cultural poverty of the pre-Islamic 'Age of Ignorance'. The spirit of Islam was not rational in the Greek sense of the term, in that God was beyond Reason and His ordering of the Universe was to be accepted not explained. True knowledge is that of God and His Law, which embraces all human activity. This is an important ingredient in Islamic thinking from the start, which later became more explicit in countering heresy and enthroning orthodoxy.[1] Truth was to be sought only in divine revelation.

Yet after the Mongol devastation, Islam set out on a new expansion for 400 years (1300–1700) — a second age of conquest and empire from Hungary to Indonesia. Four illustrious states adorned the Muslim world: Mamluk Egypt, Ottoman Turkey, Safavid Persia and Mogul India. But this second imperial age differed from the first in that the Arabs were now subjects not masters (which is why they do not like it; for Arabs today the Golden Age of Islam ended in 1258), and they played little or no part in the new states.

The last 300 years (since 1700) have been dismal for Islam. The Mamluks were eliminated in 1798 by European power, the Safavids were extinguished in 1723 and the Moguls around the same time, and the Ottomans in 1918. The greatest devastators of Islam have been the liberal West and autocratic Russia.

Despite the recent political emancipation of these areas there is as yet no sense of Muslim unity or even a genuine Renaissance; only a resurgence and militancy, just as diverse as the political and religious experience of Muslims in an earlier period in their history. Perhaps because since the eleventh century, the only political theory of Islam has been that of passive obedience to any *de facto* authority, government by consent remains an unknown concept; autocracy has been the real and, in the main, the only experience.[2]

Lacking the humanist and scientific tradition and recognizing their cultural and material backwardness, Muslims are attracted and repelled by the West at one and the same time. The Muslim traditional, quietist conservative and the more radical, activist militant alike, however, still believe that ultimate truth and wisdom rest in superior Islam, not in the inferior West. With this brief, captious but necessary recapitulation of the Islamic historical experience, we can now turn to a consideration of the rather wide subject of Islam and the nation-state. The brief is too broad and unmanageable if one is to throw some light on the relation between a faith and a civilization on the one hand and an organization of power, an arrangement for a public order on the other. One must therefore confine one's exposition to a highly selective array of concepts, relations, problem areas and illustrations, if one is to convey both the historical evolution of religion and state in Islam as well as its significance today, and the way it manifests itself in the affairs of states whose populations happen to be Muslim in the main but which are not necessarily Islamic states; or of nation-states that are not quite nations in the secular sense of the term. This in turn will force us to consider terms, definitions, perceptions and interpretations.

In looking at the central political notions in the Islamic scripture, the Koran, or the structure of political ideas that one can extrapolate from it, my colleague Michael Cook suggests that one can form a general view of their import. For the believers, these ideas basically suggest that there are those who rule and those who are ruled: the weak, the oppressed. The meek shall not inherit the earth, unless they get up and go, or emigrate (*muhajirun*), in order to constitute a political community, with a designated authority — the Prophet or Caliph — membership of which is sharply defined in religious terms: believers versus unbelievers (*kuffar*), with an intermediate category of hypocrites (*munafiqun*). There is one clear political activity for the members of the community: *jihad*, or holy war, against unbelievers who are outside it.

The Koranic conception of politics is not irenic. It is confrontationist, or rather Manichean, emphasizing rectitude versus error, and an armed confrontation between them. It is also radically monotheistic, synthesizing a monotheist policy *ex nihilo*. Moreover, the political idiom of the Koran itself is ideological.[3] Thus the unbelievers are enemies of God (see Khomeini), who are pitted against the believers, who are friends of God (and the Ayatollah).[4] The actions of believers are couched in sacred terms: *jihad, hijra* (migration), etc.

What the Koran has to say about politics is not tied to a specific historical context and is therefore widely applicable. Thus, *jihad* is a most amenable notion to the purposes of state: it can legitimize aggressive policy. But Koranic political ideas provide no clear-cut blueprint for authority in the Islamic community after the Prophet; the Koranic term *imam* does not refer to a ruler, but a prayer leader. *Amir al-muminin* (Commander of the Faithful) is not a Koranic term, but shares with the Koran the ideological overtone of militancy. The term *khalifa* (Vicegerent) appears in the Koran but not as *khalifatullah* (Vicegerent of God); rather, it denotes broadly the Muslims at large as inheritors of the earth.

The basic structure of political ideas in the Koran, though activist and militant, is somewhat neutral and does not help the rule of the Islamic community after the Prophet. However, these ideas remain equally dangerous and uncomfortable for the Muslim rulers because they are ideological. They can be mobilized equally in the conflict against unbelievers and against Muslim rulers, as indeed they have.

On the whole, the Koran is a meagre source on political authority in Islam. Muhammad derived his political power from a divine office, but the new concept of *amir al-muminin* afterwards produced a disparity between the way that accession to power occurred historically and the theory of the Caliphate, or leadership of the Islamic community, evolved by jurists — or the way in which *ijma'*, the consensus of the community, justified whatever happened in Islam; or the constant psychological problem of the dichotomy between the real and the ideal, between God's dominion and the observance of the law; or the division of legal authority between a temporal and religious official class, the sultans and the *ulema*, and the new extra-canonical sources of law, such as custom, convention and the ruler's will (*qanun, nizam, iradeh*). Political authority in Islam, therefore, is not simply based on Koranic sources. Other traditional, cultural and environmental influences, such as tribalism, Byzantine-type despotism, Iranian-style court practices and later Turkish autocracy also helped to shape it.[5]

Another colleague, Patricia Crone, has argued recently that Muhammad was a militant preacher, who combined possession of the Word of God with a particularistic ethnos — the Arab tribal communities of Arabia — to produce a dynamic for the conquest of the region, without any prior political tradition.[6] The only thing the Peninsula Arabs possessed was ethnic and cultural homogeneity. But the whole movement which became the basis of a new civilization was born in the mind of one man — Muhammad. Having united the feuding Arab tribes into one community based on the Word of God as revealed to one of them, conquest in the name of this God became possible. In short, a particular insular tribal society went out to conquer in the name of a universal truth or faith.

The problem of religion and state was born with this curious 'marriage' between a universal religious truth or message and an otherwise very parochial community which held it and fought for it or in its name. Establishing and legitimizing an Islamic state in settled non-tribal communities proved impossible. In other words, as conquerors, the early Muslim Arabs broke out everywhere with a common identity, but without the structures for a state. Whatever instruments they took over — bureaucracies, courts, mercenary and slave professional armies — all served to keep them in power. Once they lost their own military power to the new groups of mercenary and slave armies recruited by the Caliphs to fight their wars, the very nature of their political order was transformed beyond all recognition, first into a military polity and later into a military-bureaucratic one. Inevitably, the distance between religion and state grew, without however — beyond the well-known juristic rationalizations — reformulating the relationship. Thus, 'power in Islam had to be intrinsically sacred: it was only when power and sanctity no longer could be kept together that the Muslims had to make do with an illusion'.[7]

In dealing with religion and state we are therefore in a sense dealing not merely with a serious practical problem of government and politics but also with a theoretical fiction.

Power in the community and the state in Islam originally derived from an ethnic faith. To this extent Muslims have been unwilling to share the power given to them by God with others. They exclusively possess religious truth and power, as per, for instance, the Koranic Sura: 'Power belongs to God, His Apostle, and the believers.'[8] Nor did they combine at the beginning learning and power; this combination was left to non-Arab converts who greatly influenced the development of the civilization of Islam but hardly changed its general character, particularly as regards the relation between religion and state.

The reshaping of Islamic government on the Persian model, for instance, continued to be rejected or ignored by Arab Muslims. It produced bureaucratic, fiscal and other government functions, all separate from the original intention of the fusion of power and sanctity. The *ulema* who were most adamant in rejecting the desanctification of power ended up as the guardians of the religious law, but hardly helped either the retention of the old fusion or the move towards 'two worlds', the temporal and the spiritual. Whereas the Christians in Europe were, by the fourteenth to fifteenth centuries, defining temporal power as vain and transient, they none the less accepted it. The Muslims, under the guidance of their *ulema*, simply rejected temporal power, which was very much with them, as illegitimate. To this extent they perpetuated the illusion or fiction and yet kept the religious law hopelessly tied to secular power. Sacred title to power by Islamic rulers, underpinning the legitimacy of their rule, remained in the face of its having been acquired by force. The jurists and scribes continued to insist, as Ibn Muqaffaʿ did, that the Caliph was the sole source of religious and political authority, and therefore he must impose religious and political uniformity on community and polity.[9]

As the central political authority grew and expanded its

functions, recourse to the creation of slave institutions to control and govern it completed the separation between caliphal authority and power. The state, in effect, ceased to lay claim to religious authority which ended in the exclusive hands of the *ulema*. State power however was often shared by local satraps, notables, dynasties and others. The rest of the burgeoning urban society, concerned with commercial and other wealth, became non-political. The separation of central power and society ensued.[10] In fact, more and more groups in society, if not society in its entirety, avoided the state, so that a disjunction occurred between the exponents of state authority and those of religion.

Subsequently, new or fresh conquerors of infidel lands in the name of Islam came to be considered defenders of the faith. Even though most of them may have been usurpers, they nevertheless acquired Islamic legitimacy, and their power the halo or illusion of sanctity. Such were, for example, the Ottomans. No wonder then that states, in the sense of *dawla* or dynasties, rose and declined, or appeared and disappeared, ruling over societies that remained fairly stable for a long time.

One of the practical consequences of both the sanctity of power and the historical separation of state and society has been the problem of communalism, in the religious sectarian and ethnic sense. There is thus sectarianism within the Islamic community itself, occasioned by the major split between Sunni (orthodox) and Shii (or heterodox) Islam. Further sectarian proliferation is reflected in the several variants of both orthodox and heterodox Islam: Kharijites, or Ibadis, Zaidis, Ismailis, Alawis, Nusayris and Druzes. More problematic and conflict-generating has been the division between Muslim and Christian communities in the region, with a parallel rampant sectarianism within the latter too. The ethnic fragmentation has been equally problematic: Kurds, Turcomans, Circassians and others.

Since the Middle East has always been a mosaic, a kaleidoscope of co-existing sectarian and ethnic communities, any strengthening of integrative nationalist or dominant religio-political movements inevitably brings the problem of ethnic and/or religious minorities to the surface. This has been a recurring phenomenon, more recently in the inter-war period, and today in Lebanon, Syria, Iran and even Egypt.

In the absence of civil polities — in the sense of political orders in which the identity, rights and duties of the individual *vis-à-vis* the state are set out by and in impersonal constitutional, legislative and other institutional arrangements or devices — a commonly understood concept of citizenship, irrespective of religious, ethnic or other distinguishing differences, is difficult to establish and apply uniformly.

Moreover, in polities where the state, or authority, and political power — even legitimacy — is partly justified by reference to religion or religious belief, integral citizenship, given religious and ethnic diversity, is problematic at best.

Most of the constitutions of these states today proclaim Islam as the official state religion. One can point to the practice of the toleration of religious minorities as a tradition in the Islamic polity. It is not the same however as defining full citizenship without reference to religion or its tolerant attitude. One of the difficulties is that Islam does not recognize an existence for man independent of religion, because it does not entertain a Law of Nature that can be discovered by human reason, nor does it distinguish between nature (*physis*) and law (*nomos*). Consequently, man can have no rights that derive from a man-made, or positive, law, nor ones that are sanctioned by a Natural Law of reason independently of the revealed religious law. Law and nature are one, because God controls the universe and everything in it in the divine pattern He has revealed to the believers in the Holy Book and, by extension, in the revealed Sacred Law. It is difficult, therefore, when the official religion of the state is Islam, for non-Muslims to enjoy secularly based rights beyond those allowed by the traditional practice of the toleration of the 'People of the Book', i.e. those who have a holy scripture.

The activity of militant Islamic groups which aims at the establishment of an Islamic state and the resurgence of Islamic militancy throughout the Middle East tend to exacerbate the communal problem. The reaction of minorities can be equally terrifying and disruptive. The example of sectarian groups in Lebanon, Syria, Iran and even Egypt challenging the structures and authority of the state and resorting to paramilitary means to reassert their identity are cases in point. But it is also a response to a so-called national policy which appeals more to religious sanction for its authority (both for domestic and external reasons). The cumulative outcome of these developments has been witnessed in the last decade.

The demand by militant religious groups that the state realize and implement God's pattern for the Universe which He controls, as revealed to the believers through the Prophet, and their willingness to challenge the authority of that state by force (in fact, the state has already made concessionary gestures towards them: e.g. recognizing the religious law as the main source of state legislation), or in other words, the desire and willingness to fight for a monolithic — an ideological — state, based on religious doctrine, by definition invites a communal and sectarian problem when the non-Muslim native minority constitutes between three and five per cent of the population in the region.

We need not even argue the proposition that religious militancy tends to be exclusive in its political implications for state and society. Or, as Albert Camus put it, when politics becomes religion, it is the Inquisition. The fact remains that no strictly secular principle of consensus (not to say, ideology) has been devised in the countries that can resolve the matter. It is inevitable that, as the current struggle between established authority and militant religious groups continues, the spectre of the communal problem will haunt many of these countries; not just as regards Christian or other minorities, but also the Islamic majority, as one observes today in Iran and Syria — even Lebanon if the recent Shii-Sunni bloodletting is considered. Within the latter it generally manifests itself as the struggle between the transcendentalists and moderates on the one side, and the militant immanentists on the other.

The following propositions may be included in a consideration of religion and state:

(1) The extent to which the authority of the state is legitimized by a religious referrent and, by extension, the degree to which religion serves as an ideology for the political order;

(2) The extent to which the nexus of 'religion and state' implies a necessary connection between religious and political identity; that is, that the individual has no political identity and hardly any political rights other than those which derive from his religious faith, or which are independent of his religious status and belief;

(3) The relation of the official religious establishment to the state;

(4) The constitutional and legal implications of the relation between religion and state;

(5) The weight and importance given to religion by the state;

(6) The degree to which any peculiar relation between state and religion undermines or even precludes a civil polity;

(7) The communal problem or problems the relation may give rise to.

These general propositions by no means exhaust the list of implications in the relation between religion and state. The fact that seven are listed should not be interpreted as a preference for or an attachment to any mystical, esoteric neo-Pythagorean or other cultish beliefs and practices.

Nor should one assume that the issue of religion and state is a recent preoccupation in the study of any society where the faith of Islam predominates. The recurring problem of this difficult and unresolved relation derives from the confusion over it in early Islam. In fact, it has been echoed in modern times over such issues as the Caliphate in the twenties;[11] the sources of legislation ever since the 'modern' states in the Middle East were created; Islamic versus secular government and culture; the meaning of the faith as distinguished from religious thought;[12] the failure of Islamic reform; constitution-making; the split between quietistic transcendental official Islam on the one hand and a popular religion — occasionally transformed into a militant, activist populist one, with the sectarian or communal problem inherent in the relationship — on the other.

The Islamic faith has social and political significance, centred on the paramount notion of the community (*umma*) as the expression of a religious idea. The community exists in order for the believers to actualize the Islamic ideal: God's revealed pattern for the universe. This is clearly a dynamic revolutionary recipe which explains in part the emphasis on force and the community in Islamic militancy today. If one coupled this to the Muslim conception of history as a series of revelations culminating with the final perfect one — that of Islam to Muhammad — it is not only the implication for the problem of change which is significant but also the suggestion that the earlier political, earthly success of the community vindicated the revelation. The subsequent disparity between the idealized Islamic history and the actual history of Islamic society exercises the Muslim and moves him toward regeneration in two directions: against internal decay and against external threats actual or perceived, or domination, and in this way he resists the further disintegration of Islam's temporal greatness. Mundane history in fact must be subordinated to the revelation. The original message and the presumed classical ideal model remain the norm.

The Muslim's supreme duty is less to know the truth and more to do right; that is why the law, or *sharia*, is really at the heart of Islamic culture. But it is also his duty — the immanentist aspect of his faith — to realize God's divine pattern on earth. The task of the Muslim today is not to seek the truth, but to restore power. This is the significance of the Muslim Brotherhood in Egypt and the Islamic militant organizations in Pakistan and Iran. They all wish to make Islam the operative force in society and the organizing principle of politics; they want to elicit loyalty and action, to activate the faithful by re-politicizing religion. The state, both in Islam and according to these groups, is a religious, not a territorial or ethnic, concept. It is even ideological, because it views political power as a means of attaining the religious ideal, i.e. the unfettered application of the *sharia*. Pakistan has, since its inception in 1947, claimed that it aims to make Islam the social ideal of the *umma*, an independent political community as the arena for religious activity. The state will exist so that the Islamic norm will apply to its life and public affairs. That Pakistan, Iran or Saudi Arabia represent forms of Islam there is no doubt. But whether they represent Islamic states as a particular form of state is doubtful. No one knows exactly what an Islamic state looks like; we simply know of states that are Muslim. That there is an ideal Islamic state is arguable, but that there is an actual state in the form of an Islamic state is problematic and controversial. Hence the recurrent debate about religion and state since the 1920s in Egypt, or Turkey before that, and the continuing controversy over whether Islam is only a religion or both religion and state.[13]

There is a difference between Islam serving as a guide and inspirational ideal of authority or a political order, and Islam with its law, the *sharia* being the constitution of the state, or the organizing principle of authority and basis of legitimacy. The fact remains that the core of the faith is the terrestrial expression of the divine message; that is, Islam is by definition a political religion: it presumes political duties for the believers. A way out was proposed by E.I.J. Rosenthal, when he suggested nearly 20 years ago that an Islamic state is pure *sharia* and unattainable, whereas a Muslim state has been historically feasible, because the functions of authority are divided between the sultan, wielder of secular power, and the *ulema*, interpreters of the religious message and guardians of the sacred law. Such a state is based on Islamic principles but not exclusively on the *sharia*, which is not in control of the body politic.

Extreme Muslims such as Abu al-Ala' al-Mawdudi and Muhammad Asad have put forward the theory of a state as an ideological community which excludes non-Muslims.[14] If Islam is to serve only as a religious and moral force in a modern lay state, the difficulties are not great, but if the *sharia* is to be exclusively applied, it would not be binding on those who do not profess the faith. Communal problems arise. The fact remains that theoretically the word of God is the sole provision for civil organization; God is the sole sovereign and legislator. Unlike Christianity, Islam renders belief a value of the political order; in fact, the only true value which gives the earthly city its *raison d'être*. The *umma* becomes the only community, or nation, that has a right to exist on earth. The opposition of the righteous against the sinner, or the believer against the infidel, implies that no unbelieving entity can be tolerated. If the Islamic state is needed for the realization of God's message, then citizenship is not based on *jus sanguinis* or *jus solis* but on *jus religionis*.

Serious problems arise when one realizes that Islam is indissolubly religion *and* community, or nation, and it demands that this combination or duality be inscribed in temporal structures. As a religion, it is not a detached private affair; it is rather closer to the medieval conception: it determines man's whole being, his identity and status. Nor is the *umma* a church; it is a society of believers, comprising those who profess Islam, pray to the *qibla*, observe the *sharia* and preferably live in *dar al-islam*. Its unity is and is not strictly political. Its law is a decision of divine will; there is no other source of law, including Nature and Reason. Religious and social ethics are equated, so that there is no dichotomy between man the individual in relation to family and society — or the member of a political organization — on the one hand, and man expressing himself in religious terms about God on the other. God is the Lord of the Universe and the earth is His lawful realm; a kind of secular and eschatological notion simultaneously. The purpose of Islam, as Professor Gibb argued over thirty years ago, is to make it dominant in every sphere of life.[15]

In dealing with the question of whether Islam can become the foundation of a political order, one must remember that, unlike developments in the West, Islam emphasizes the community, not the individual, and religious belief is simultaneously other- and this-worldly; that is, transcendent or eschatological and immanent at one and the same time. Moreover, it seeks a unitary not a plural civilization and political culture. Hence the perennial problem of reconciling the claims of a universal *umma*, or nation, with the demands and needs, the reality indeed, of several Muslim states and later territorially-defined 'nation-states'. There is, theoretically, no separation of religion and power. Western Christians viewed temporal power as transient and therefore accepted it as unrelated to their religious belief. At the same time, this separation salvaged some of the Christian ethic even for the most crass of secularists.

But as I already indicated, this pure or extreme Islamic position can be held only if one overlooks, the concrete events of mundane Islamic history. Islam as a religion may have remained strong, but it lost its force as the arbiter of much of the social, but certainly most of the political, life and order a long time ago. It is for this reason that Muslims today can assert that the spiritual recovery of Islam is only possible with the reassertion of its political strength. But they gloss over the nature of rule as it evolved in Islamic history.[16]

The basis of all Muslim thought about religion and society is the Koran, the direct word of God; and the Muslim state must be the political expression and instrument of this Koranic orthodoxy. The *ulema* interpret it in the form of a transcendent unitarian orthodoxy, while historically the ruler ignored and bypassed it with his secular ordinances, laws and decrees. Similarly, people escaped it by resorting either to custom and convention or to mystical sufism. Its emphasis on the community rendered personal religious experience, outside intuitive pantheist mysticism, difficult. As a result, it has always been difficult to deal with the historic community. Similarly, the social tradition of the community has been so massively powerful that individualism has suffered. One has heard of a Muslim mystic, but not of a Muslim ascetic.

Because religion and philosophy have been irreconcilable in the face of the power of revelation, reform movements in recent times have failed, and all liberal experiments have foundered on the rock of absolutism. Several paradoxes regarding authority developed. An aversion to rationalism accompanied the idea of a transcendent all-powerful God. Consequently, abstract concepts of nature, justice and law were rejected. The emphasis has been on the externality of rules, formalism in law and a corpus of tradition. The absolute equality of believers became juxtaposed with the development of autocratic rule. The absence of natural rights rendered freedom a juridical, not a metaphysical, concept. As the servant of God, man was ontologically nothing. Whereas the concept of the nation rested on the principle of the equality and brotherhood of believers, there was no place for the concept of liberty. And all this juridical structure was based on the idea of a covenant (*'ahd*), not on natural values outside the formal, Koranic ones. Even the so-called consensus of the community (*ijma'*) remained a construct of divine will, not even of a mythical popular, or societal, will. The only political theory possible therefore has been a juridical one, without reference to the nature of man. Freedom meant what was offered by the covenant of the *umma*; for non-Muslims it was supplied by the idea of toleration (*dhimma*) and protection (*aman*).

As the fundamental bases of the faith, the Koran, Tradition and consensus of the community led to a kind of totalitarian scholasticism and political authoritarianism, under which consensus as the expression of *vox populi* was not a liberal principle but one of authority. Much of this, as Gibb argued, occurred when a fundamentalist doctrine was pitted against independent intellectual activity, especially after the rejection of Greek rationalism. No wonder then that any theory of knowledge became dominated by the idea of authority, and knowledge itself remained a solid immobile mass instead of a dynamic instrument. The mystics were no help either, since knowledge for them was intuition. It is possibly what might have happened to Western Christianity had it not succumbed to Greek humanism and science and Roman law. Legal science emphasizes Islam's rejection of any utilitarian ethic. The science of law became the 'knowledge of rights and duties whereby man is enabled to observe right conduct in this life and to prepare himself for the world to come'.[17] By its nature, law became bound up with religious ethic. It was not regarded like Christian and Roman law as the 'gradual deposit of people's historical experience'. Its primary function was to classify action in terms of absolute standards of good and evil; all else is secondary.

The argument that society cannot be stable unless it is permeated by religious belief, may even suggest a totalitarian system of ideas. Islam is the only religion that has consistently aimed to construct a society on this principle through the instrument of the *sharia*: an instrument by which the social ethic of Islam is consolidated, but which excludes politics, administration and commerce. These areas of human activity were left to non-religious elements. Eventually there was a bifurcation, a dichotomy between the natural historical development of these aspects of Islamic life and the theoretical religious ideal adhered to by the nation. The sultanate, based on power, was accepted in lieu of the caliphate for the sake of social peace (Ibn Jamaa, Mawardi, al-Ghazali).[18] And this has been the foundation of the state in the Islamic world more or less since. As the political obligation of obedience remained a religious duty, the legitimacy of the ruler could be rationalized or justified as necessary for the existence and perpetuation of the *umma* (Sura xxii:22), who protects and enforces the sacred law, in order to lead Muslims to prosperity in this world and salvation in the next.[19] The law's main aim remained the prevention of evil by a blend of legal and moral principles, but the political system comprised the *umma* and a ruler who was only formally a spiritual-religious guide.

A public order whose principle is personified in God, and a community whose foundation for observing right conduct is the *sharia*, made submission to it both a duty and a precept of faith. Its violation was both a dereliction, or violation, of duty and a sin. Historically, the beneficiaries of this demanding precept have been rulers whose very possession of power rendered them legitimate. This is also how a huge body of Traditions and a variety of practices were not simply viewed as part of the Tradition but were incorporated as integral parts of the faith.

A basic ingredient of the current Islamic movement in its challenge of existing orders is the rejection of such unconditional political obligation in the name of the ideal Islamic polity, in which power and sanctity are once again fused. But an equally important ingredient of this movement — perhaps the only tangible one — is a very mundane struggle for power and the control of the state.

2

Islam and the Nation-State: An Enduring Contradiction

The entry for 'Nation' in the *International Encyclopedia of the Social Sciences* (1968) asserts that 'nation' is now accepted as a central political concept of recent times, and that it is either synonymous with a state or its inhabitants, or a human group bound together by loyalty and common solidarity. This suggests that a nation-state is a territorial entity in which the state is co-extensive with the nation. Nationalism on the other hand is the desire to form and maintain a state, and often precedes the emergence of the nation, as in Fichte's *Address to the German Nation* (1808), the writings of Arab nationalists, the Phil-hellenic movement and the Italian Risorgimento in the nineteenth century, the Ali Jinnah call for a Muslim state of Pakistan in the 1940s, etc. Nationality, moreover, emerged in northern and western Europe by the eighteenth century, securely based on a continuity of political rule by dynasties and governing elites as far back as the Middle Ages. It became the basic determinant of political identity and loyalty. In some instances, as in France and America, nation and country for purposes of identity and loyalty are synonymous, so that classifying peoples into nations and making this their primary basis of corporate political identity was until recently a Western European practice. Elie Kedourie has argued that nationalism is a doctrine invented in Europe, by which humanity was divided into nations, defined by their history, language, etc., and entitled to form sovereign states.[1]

When this doctrine travelled eastwards after Napoleon, or was imported into the Middle East, it became precarious, because it clashed with older, deeper loyalties, and remained insignificant in determining political identity and directing political loyalty under Islam. A country in Islamic history is a place, and a nation is a people, or the *umma*, the community determined by religious belief, i.e. the nation of believers. Identity remained based on religious belief and loyalty developed, by force of historical circumstances, to a state, a government, or a ruler.

The nation-state emerged in the West when the connotation of religion had been limited to one aspect of the individual's life, separated from its other aspects. In Islam the connotation of religion is wider, encompassing both the private and public aspects of the individual's life, because the religious law of God applies to the entire human activity. Thus in the West the nation-state as a basic unit can comprise different religious communities; in Islam the religious community is the basic unit or the nation, comprising historical states. Religion remained the determinant of political identity, the focus of loyalty and the source of authority.

To what extent may one argue that the absence of the term 'state', let alone 'nation-state', from the Islamic and more modern Middle Eastern vocabulary indicates the absence of the idea of a legitimate sovereignty as an impersonal public rule with a right to govern over a particular political community and territory? The term *dawla* is a fairly recent one. As a concept it referred in the recent past to a ruler's administration or a dynasty of rulers — e.g. the *dawla* of Muhammad Ali in Egypt — as did the concept of Sultanate as for example the Ottoman Empire. The notion of sovereignty (*siyada*), however derived or achieved, may have been implicit in the term *dawla*, but not institutionally expressed or embodied. Similarly, neither was 'legitimacy', which was often claimed by force and conquest, giving rise to the political dictum or aphorism in Islamic tradition, that the 'powerful must be obeyed' [*man ishtaddat waṭ'aṭuhu wajabat ta'aṭuhu*]. Although in Muhammad's new *umma*, the political community of believers in Medina, the new faith of Islam, preceded all other loyalties, the Prophet did not abolish the existing tribal-constitutional arrangement. His so-called Medina Constitution created a new political community— legislation which was limited to his own lifetime role as arbiter (*hakam*). Thus, ultimate authority or legitimacy for acts of the community rested not with the tribal chiefs as before, but with the one deity, Allah, and His Prophet, Muhammad. Was this tantamount to a new concept of a *sovereign overlord*? A new

Leviathan? It suggested, in any case, that Muhammad derived his political authority in Medina at least from the divine nature of his prophetic function. It is significant that after his death, his successors, the first caliphs, introduced a new 'sovereign' concept, that of *amir al-muminin*, Commander of the Faithful (or Believers).

This new concept produced yet another contradiction or dichotomy. To begin with, there was the disparity between the way accession — and succession — to power occurred historically, and the theory of the Caliphate/Imamate — the leadership of the Muslim community (*umma*) — as evolved by Muslim jurists, for example, al-Mawardī.[2] Even the election of the *imam* by *ahl al'aqd wa'l-ḥall* meant in practice election by the influential and powerful in the community. Similarly, appointment/designation by the sitting Caliph/*imam* was usually approved or confirmed by the consensus (*ijma'*) of the community, i.e. the consensus of the *ulema* and religious jurists. Finally, the acquiescence of the wider community justified whatever happened in Islam; in other words, whatever the ruler, together with the influential, the powerful and the 'religious teachers', did.

In any case, the state in Western Europe as an expression of political reality and an impersonal source of public law, is a relatively recent institution, which even now holds sway over a limited territory. But this too is an alien proposition to Islam. State and government as they emerged in early Islam, and particularly Arab-dominated Islam, did so as personal and dynastic concepts. Whereas the European-centred concept of the nation-state requires the identification of a people — a national-cultural group in a defined territory — the Islamic state emphasizes the dynastic basis or foundation regarding the relation (or link) of political power to group feeling and/or identity. After all, the *umma* of Muhammad or Islam, the community of the faithful, is not exactly a nation in the European or national(ist) sense. Rather, it designates a group of people, a community, that has been the special object of divine revelation, i.e. the recipient of a divine message. The nation-state, moreover, implies territory with a people and a government. The nearest equivalent early Arabic-Islamic term for people is perhaps *sha'b*, a people so designated by the territorial principle, who inhabit a particular territory. National/political identity in early Islam, however, emphasized ancestry and genealogy, a natural outcome of its tribal provenance and society, or social environment. To this extent the genealogical concept of identity is associated with the Arab Muslims, clearly because of its importance in tribal society, whereas the popular (*sha*ʿ*b*)-territorial one is associated with non-Arab Muslims, such as the Iranian-Sassanid (ʿ*ajam*) who were a people (*sha*ʿ*b*) with a defined or specific territorial domicile.

In his classic work, *al-*ʿ*Iqd al-farid*, Ibn Abd Rabbihi (860–940) alludes to the earliest controversy regarding the nation and, by extension today, the nation-state. This was pitted against the genealogical principle and came to be known as *shu*ʿ*ubiyya*, or a non-Arab popular territorial political movement against the Arab-dominated central Islamic political authority or power. *Shu*ʿ*ubi* became a pejorative term in Islam's political vocabulary, referring to the cultural territorial-based separatist movements for autonomy, usually by non-Arab Muslims 'who had kings to unite them before Islam, cities which gathered them [i.e. lived in particular localities], and secular [i.e. non-Islamic] laws ante-dating the *Sharia* which they obeyed'.[3] Two kinds of contradictory loyalties are recognized here: the religious and the local/territorial.

The nation-state is thus a concept alien to Islam. And if the impersonal legitimate sovereignty of government arises from popular consent, this is equally difficult in Islam. The idea of the nation-state therefore remains a European import at variance with the tradition of Islam.

Today there are states which are predominantly Muslim but which, even though not nation-states, are nevertheless recognized by international bodies as sovereign within territorial boundaries. Several of them are successors to more traditional relations of dominance, but surrounded or propped up by a scaffolding of European-style institutions and claiming legitimacy partly on the basis of imported ideologies. Neither the scaffolding nor the ideology can lay claim to native provenance or spontaneity. Whatever their justifications in borrowed ideology or institutions, these states, so far, have been unable to meet, let alone counter, the challenge of the native political idiom and perception, that of Islam.

Having noted these anomalies, one must, even if only as a matter of convenience in political discourse, use the term state in the Islamic context. The term nation-state remains misleading. Even in Europe, nations and states were rarely coterminous.

States, or sovereigns, required the fairly recent ideological underpinning of nationalism to persist with the idea of the nation-state.

However, even in the earlier periods, successive Muslim rulers and governments — like the Prophet himself in Medina — allowed local influences in religious practice. In many instances, local custom and pre-Islamic traditional practice, together with the arbitrary will of the ruling potentate, became the legal basis of government. Customary usage and traditional practice regulated the conduct of commercial relations and trade transactions. Although the ruler was theoretically [the agent] expected to enforce the provisions and apply the rules of the *sharia*, he more often than not legislated and governed on the basis of custom and tradition. The codifications of the *sharia* by the various schools or rites of law (the *fiqh* of the *fuqaha'*) represent an ideal pattern of conduct that was and often is overriden by local custom, usage and tradition. Thus the law of blood vengeance (*al-tha'r*), which is really revenge. No wonder that in all periods of Islamic history, the *sharia* and its several codifications have been disregarded and ignored in so many respects. Hence the ambivalence of Muslims towards the Sacred Law from the start. Both the Koran and the *sunna* of the Prophet became virtually obsolete as practical guides to living within a generation of the Prophet's death, or by 660–1, upon the first civil war in the Muslim community. The *sharia* remained the ideal rule for model Islamic conduct, to be implemented only under the rule of the expected *mahdi*, the Divinely Guided Imam. The disparity between the real and the ideal in Islam, including legal conduct, constituted a serious psychological problem for the believers. Similarly, the duty of the community to *jihad* (holy war) compounded the confusion.

In the eleventh-twelfth centuries, the great scholar Imam al-Ghazali (d.1111) put forward a widely acceptable formulation which would render the acts of secular power valid in the eyes of Islam and the Muslims. These were the ordnances and acts of the ruler (*ahkam, siyasa*) that were allowed on the basis of expediency. Eventually, legal authority was shared between the secular ruler (Sultan) and religious officials, *imams*, jurists and generally the doctors of religious sciences who interpreted the *sharia*. What it meant in practice is that the fiat of the Sultan became buttressed by the justificatory rationalization of the religious teacher. The interpreter of the Sacred Law supplied the needed legitimacy to whoever held and wielded power.[4]

This suggests a variety of extra-canonical sources of law, which became widespread and familiar under the Ottomans. An Ottoman sultan acquired the right to legislate by combining imperial will, local custom and tradition with political expediency, independent of the *ulema*, that is, without the approval of the men of religion. For instance, he could, in consultation with his ministers, express his royal will in *niẓam* (order) and *qanun* (statute), i.e. in secular legal acts. He could even express his royal will in an arbitrary way via an *irade saniya* (royal wish) or in a *firman*.

The gulf between the real and the ideal, or the Islamic ideal and the necessity of the reality of the Muslim community's historical experience, was first observed when the earliest complex administrative aspect of Islamic government was the fiscal one. Much of this arose from the distribution and disposition of conquered lands, taxation and related sources of revenue. The collection of revenues became as major and central a function of the Muslim ruler as the defence of the faith, the leadership of the Friday prayer, the conduct of *jihad*, and the overall administration and implementation of the *sharia*.

Although, again theoretically, the ruler was not allowed to legislate, he none the less had great leeway in such matters as fiscal policy, the conferment of public office and the conduct of external relations. He was also allowed great leeway in administering the temporal realm or earthly affairs of the Muslim community, state and empire.

As the writ of the central power or ruler extended over the expanding empire, so its functions expanded in order to control more areas and aspects of Muslim life and society. The fiscal power increased at a time when there was no clear distinction between the privy purse of the Caliph or *imam* and the *bait el-mal*, or public treasury. The Caliph, *imam* or ruler controlled both; so much so that the historian Ibn al-Athir was moved to describe the traditional view of public office as the path to enrichment and wealth largely as a result of extortion from the subjects; while al-Jahiz described every official as corrupt.[5] *Sharia* judges dealt only with religious matters, so that all executive decisions were left to the secular ruler, the Amir, the Sultan, that is, the prince. In these circumstances, political patronage, nepotism and corruption in the disposition of land and public office became rampant.

The nation-state could have developed during the second period of the great Islamic historical enterprise, with the rise of the Ottoman dynasty, the Safavids in Persia and the Mamluks in Egypt. For one may argue that there was in Turkey, Egypt and Persia a pre-Islamic identity, separate from, or at least antedating, Islam. It did not, because the opportunity to separate the temporal from the spiritual was not taken. Rather, as in the earlier period, both the relationship and the dichotomy were rationalized.

Instead, what happened was that the Islamic community was divided into separate political entities giving rise to states not nations, as integrative coercive power structures in the community. Within or below these states there persisted several units of identity on the basis of sect, ethnos and tribe. Inevitably, we have witnessed throughout the history of the region the persistence of the satraps, despots and other rulers, and the recurring recrudescence of local or lesser loyalties in sectarian, ethnic and communal conflict. (For example, Kurds in Iraq, Iran and Turkey; Azerbaijanis and Baluchis in Iran; pagans and Christians in southern Sudan; Druzes and Maronites in the Lebanon.)

The idea of the nation-state came to the Middle East from Europe defining for the first time the state by territory, language and descent, common national identity and common political loyalty. In the cases of Egypt, Iran and Turkey, the notion did not prove as problematic as, say, among the majority of the Arabic-speaking Middle East. The Turks managed to crystallize a nationality in contrast to a religious community and, under Atatürk, established an identity determined by national frontiers. Needless to say, they had had the advantage of a long experience of political sovereignty and a willingness to divest Islam of and deny it any role in public policy and disestablish it as a state religion. The Persians, at least in Iran, could mobilize the historical memory of an ancient monarchy, a continuity of an Iranian identity ante-dating Islam, and even a separatist Islam based on their heterodox Shii state religion, since the sixteenth century. The Egyptians, in contrast to other Arabic-speaking communities at the end of the Great War, had a stronger sense of continuity with the past, a monumental reminder of their unity and homogeneity in the pyramids and the Nile Valley, and over one hundred years of virtual autonomy from the Commander of the Faithful in Istanbul. For the remaining Arabs of the Fertile Crescent and North Africa, however, the adoption of the nation-state had to be nationalistic, i.e. radical, in the sense of aspiring to achieve a single Arab nation-state comprising a larger group of related nations; something like the German and Italian unification movements in the nineteenth century, or the pan-Slavism of the pre-Great War period.

In any case, the Arab heartland consisted of a number of provinces of the Ottoman Empire from the beginning of the sixteenth century, more or less directly ruled from Istanbul or by its appointed representatives, with the odd exception, as in the Lebanon, or the local coalescence around the odd strong local governor. They were created as states — the Hejaz, Iraq, Syria, Lebanon, Transjordan — by European powers, according to the latter's own wartime and post-war arrangements. The problems of political identity and loyalty therefore persisted in them, and as political entities they were perceived as states rather than as nation-states in the Western sense. Consequently, groups or movements in them have been trying ever since to find a national political identity: Arab, Phoenecian, Syrian, Assyrian and Babylonian, even briefly Pharaonic in Egypt. Such were the attempts of the Syrian Social National Party (PPS) — founded in 1932 and led by the Christian Lebanese, Antoun Saadeh — Arsuzi's League for National Action in Syria, and the Phalange in Lebanon in the mid-1930s; or of the Baath and the Nasserists in the fifties and sixties. The most persistent movement among the Muslim majority of these states has been that of Arab nationalism, at the heart of which lay no less than Islam, i.e. the religiously based identity.

The adoption of nationalism in new states arbitrarily created by foreign powers — that is, where the state is not coterminous with the nation — inevitably not only raised the question of the relation between the new doctrine and Islam, but necessarily rendered it radical, since it was expected to change the situation in such a way as to achieve a nation which forms, or constitutes, a state. Since the only way to define the Arab nation was by an emphasis on the past which is Islamic, the connection became even stronger. Yet Islam and nationalism are mutually exclusive terms. As a constructive loyalty to a territorially defined national group, nationalism has been incompatible with Islam in which the state is not ethnically or territorially defined, but is itself ideological and religious. Or, as W.C. Smith put it, the state is a religious norm: it is the home of the faithful — Pakistanis, Iranians, Arabs and others.[6] The territorial concept, that is, extends to wherever Muslims live, whereas the Muslim nation is both an ideal and one to which group loyalty is exclusively Muslim. It cannot entertain any group feeling that includes non-Muslims. And yet the Muslims in this century have tried to use nationalism, just as their predecessors in the nineteenth century used Islamic reform, to rehabilitate Islamic society without much success, because it is contrary to traditional Islamic loyalties. To this extent we are witnessing its rejection today by militant Islam.

Despite the controversies of the inter-war period, under the pressure of ongoing secularization in public affairs, most of these societies have been reluctant to abandon the idea that the state represents a divinely ordained system for the well-being of men in this world and the next. After about 15–20 years of unsuccessful concern over the Caliphate that was abolished by the Turks in 1924, they still clung, even in the face of hard reality, to the principle that Islam is the official religion of the state, that Arab nationalism, for example, is anchored in the 'mythical' Golden Age of Muslim culture. But the problem of deciding whether statehood is to be defined in exclusively religious terms or in terms of nations, in which religion is not the sole criterion of political identity, loyalty or national integration, remains unresolved. Or, as Professor Fazlur Rahman argued 15 years ago, there has not been as yet a reconciliation with the fact of the nation-state.[7] Nationality among the majority of their populations is still overshadowed by the religious community; national frontiers are still measured by religion. Cultural oneness, especially among the Arabs, is still supreme, since Islam is their greatest cultural achievement.

More significantly, all political movements since early Islam are closely associated with religion. In fact, the tenacious resistance to European conquest from North Africa to Iran and Central Asia (Abdel Qader in Algeria 1833–47, the Murids in Daghestan of the Caucuses in 1830–59, Iran in 1899–1907, the Mahdiyya in the Sudan in the 1880s and 1890s, the Senusiyya in Cyrenaica at the turn of the century, Orabi in Egypt in 1881–2) was based on the idea of the defence of Islam. The loyalties of the masses, as we can witness today from Iran to North Africa and from Central Asia to the Sudan, remain religious and local.

If the conception of the nation-state is new to the Middle East, dating only from 1919–20, nationalism as an idea and a movement among Middle Easterners — ever since its first stirrings in the late nineteenth century — has been an ambivalent reaction to Europe; one of opposition and emulation simultaneously. It served as a negative force against alien control and as a reassertion of the *umma* free of infidel power. It has shared this thrust with the earlier Islamic reform movement which sought to revitalize Islam as a means of resisting the encroachments and incursions of European power and ideas. Yet nationalism as the new ideology that was to revitalize the Islamic community in several new states failed to provide the basis of a new political identity and loyalty, or to reformulate the Muslim's relation to modernity. Instead, as E. Kedourie has argued, it transformed, say, through pan-Arabism, *mystique* into politique.[8] The vacuum in political institutions remained because borrowed structures of pluralistic politics, such as constitutionalism and parliamentarianism, were too alien and were in any case a mere scaffolding operated by the new official classes under the watchful eye of a foreign power for a very brief interlude. They did not long survive the departure of such foreign power.

A similar vacuum in political ideas persisted when the liberal values associated with European nationalism or the nation-state were never quite accepted in practice by their native purveyors and promoters nor at all by the masses, perhaps primarily because liberalism was never a force within Islam. They were left with Islam and its peculiar political tradition, as expressed by Hasan Banna of the Muslim Brotherhood, Abu al-Ala' al-Mawdudi of Pakistan, Khomeini of Iran, and others. And this is diametrically opposed to what is perceived as the intellectual and spiritual danger from the West. It became the foundation of the movement back to the Islamic polity.

The significant features of the Middle East in this century, once its societies came face to face with the modern world, have been political instability, intellectual disorientation and spiritual tension. Moreover, the new movement back to the Islamic polity — as per, say, Khomeini — is genuinely radical for it proposes a rule of the 'clergy' or religious teachers and jurists, something unknown in Muslim annals. In other words, it is the immanentist politicization of religion and the theocratization of the state. In the past, the long series of defeats at the hands of Christian Europe had undermined Muslim self-respect; not just defeat in a worldly sense, but it cast doubt on the truth of Muslim revelation itself, leading to loss of self-confidence. Nationalism and socialism as the new creeds of power were tried and found wanting, since these too, like reformism before them, foundered on the rock of absolutism. The memory was still alive, however, of an Islam vindicated by political success; it was a belief that the course of world history for a millennium from the seventh to the seventeenth century had proved the truth of the religion. Hence the relentless call ever since the 1930s for the return to an Islamic polity. Even though the spread of European ideas and techniques has been the most arresting and significant theme in the modern history of Islam, the peregrinations and disappointments of the Muslim intellect in its search for a valid amalgam between its native inheritance and the path of modern, i.e. Western, civilization, led first, briefly, to a pluralist political experiment of constitutionalism, soon thereafter to military coups, autocracy and despotism. The more popular that nationalism became,the more populist and Islamic a character it acquired.[9]

What was even more shattering was the fact that according to the European doctrine, a nation governs itself. Arabs, for example, acquired states after the Great War, but did not rule themselves for some time. One of the radical aims of nationalism therefore was self-rule. However, the assumption that nationalism does away with despotism — which was believed to result from the fact that nations are not self-governing — proved false. Equally vexed was the question of the kind of intellectual fiction, or transvaluation of values, which was created by nationalism. In the past one was a Muslim, a Cairene, a Damascene, a Saidi, a Beiruti, a Baghdadi. Under nationalism one became an Egyptian, a Syrian, a Lebanese, an Iraqi. But as this nationalism was closely linked to, nay, perhaps inseparable from, Islam, it failed to accommodate the other, i.e. the non-Muslim.

Artificial, heterogeneous, yet enduring 'modern states of Muslims' were created roughly 60 years ago. They have not been able to create national communities. Rather the proliferation of fragmented societies as states begs the question: What does it mean to be the ruler of Iran, Afghanistan, Syria, or Lebanon? They may of course last, especially since state structures — the administrative organizations of power — have been the main evolutionary pattern in Islamic history. Yet their legitimacy is in doubt as their structures are challenged by forces which belie the existence of a nation, or nations. They may well keep going until something drastic happens, as it did in Lebanon, or Afghanistan and Iran.

Repeatedly in recent history, the intellectual weakness of movements like Islamic reform and the adopted alien creeds of power, such as nationalism and socialism, prevented them from coming to grips with the problem of what it means to have a religious belief in modern conditions, dominated by complex economic factors, advanced science and technology. They have paid dearly for the earlier rejection of Greek rationalism in favour of the superior truth of revelation, when perhaps they could have tried to live with both. One of the consequences of this failure has been the reduction of Islam to a tool of power in the hands of the ruler — even under Khomeini, or especially under him. The Islamic state, to use Naipaul's recent terrifying metaphor about Pakistan today, is the 'Salt Hills of a Dream', where, one may add, thirst is the order of the day.[10] Vast demographic change, which brought the masses into politics, created the further need for rulers to mobilize them through the readiest and most attractive common denominator — religion. This need is the paradoxical outcome of the so-called Westernization of the last 150 years and the attendant spread of literacy.

Nor has nationalism been of the essence regarding forms of government or political behaviour in the Middle East. The former have been varied in the basis of their legitimacy and loyalty, ranging from religious to dynastic, tribal and sectarian. The basis of the latter remained anchored in primordial and traditional relations and loyalties. The traditional fusion in varying degrees of religion and polity has, so far, prevailed. As a doctrine, moreover, nationalism was confined to the politically articulate strata of society. The masses had no idea of the nation, nationality or even nationalism. They remained, on the whole, simply Muslim. Even the articulators of the idea, in addition to their remoteness from liberalism, have had little respect for territorial boundaries imposed by outsiders. Emphasizing territory, government and people as nationalism does, it was pitted against the long-standing Islamic tradition of ancestry, genealogy and community so closely associated with tribal societies and their religious movement. The *umma* is not a nation-state; it refers to a people or group that has been the special recipient of a divine revelation.

The North African writer Abdullah Laroui, in *The Crisis of the Arab Intellectual* asserted, 'Arab culture both in its classical expression and in the most influential aspect of its present-day expression is opposed in almost every particular to liberal culture'. Consequently, 'Arabs have been unable to provide a connection between their vision of the classical age and today [the modern age] when they are forced to succumb to a different history'. He insists that today's national state in the Middle East is dominated by the petite bourgeoisie and is controlled by a centralized power structure headed by the army and the bureaucracy. In confronting Europe, the conservatives or fundamentalists opposed Islamic culture, the pseudo-liberals put forward the nation, and the revolutionaries the class, so that the current revolutionary nationalism — including militant Islam — seems relevant to all three: a dominated nation, a threatened culture and an exploited class. One notes all the same that the Palestine question, for example, has reinforced traditional ideology and traditional political loyalties and perceptions. Thus, if Westernization caused alienation among Muslims, a parallel alienation within the community occurred with what Laroui calls medievalization; that is, the Arab's identification with the great period of the classical Golden Age of Islamic history. This led the Arab to lose his self in the absolutism of language, culture and the saga of the past; a kind of rigidity leading to *immobilisme*.

> All too long has the Arab intellectual hesitated to make radical criticism of culture, language and tradition. Too long has he drawn back from criticising aims of local national policy, the result of which is a stifling of democracy and a generalized dualism. He must condemn superficial economism, which would modernize the country and rationalize society by constructing factories with another's money, another's technology, another's administration. When it comes to problems of minorities and local democracy he must cease from censoring himself for fear of imperilling an apparent national unity. The Arab intellectual has too long applauded the call to Arab unity, while accepting and sometimes justifying the fragmentation that is reality.[11]

The traditional yearning to be ruled, to have strong leaders, is perhaps due to the fact that, historically, stability in Middle Eastern society has not been due to basic institutions, but to the networks of loyalties, kinship and patron-client relations, the status of honour, pedigree and wealth, all of which are underpinned by oaths.[12] This arrangement promoted the value of the community over that of the state or the nation. But of course it could not and did not last.

If one is to characterize the problematic nexus 'Islam and the nation-state', certain arguable propositions are possible. Significantly — and this I developed back in 1966–7, long before such a preoccupation among Western scholars was widespread — Islam is a whole tradition, comprising a religious doctrine, a juridical system, a culture and civilization, with a recorded political past. Tradition, therefore, in dealing with fundamental questions like religion and state, the community and the nation-state, is a more encompassing and useful term than religion or even Islam. It follows that the failure of religious reform in the past to reformulate the doctrine and find an acceptable formula for its accommodation with modernity, as well as the failure of the nationalist revolution to construct a nation-state based on political identity and loyalty other than that provided by religious belief, has been due to the absence of forceful rulers able to manipulate the tradition while remaining acceptable to traditional society; and equally to the failure of intellectuals to incorporate rationalism, humanism and science into the Muslim system of thought. Tradition, therefore, remained relevant to the capacity of leaders, or rulers, to act politically.

One also observes that the growing disinterestedness in Islam as a religion on the part of many Muslims has been strangely accompanied by a parallel political revival of Islam as a culture, a legacy, a tradition, linking faith once again to political duty, reviving cultural identity and regenerating local or Islamic culture, i.e. formulating an ideology. This is inexorably connected with the aspiration to power as an essential precondition of regeneration. With petro-wealth and the decline of non-Muslim power it acquired a dynamic momentum.

In its early enthusiasm, Western literature on comparative politics and the study of the developing nations referred to modernization as a universal process that had been accelerated with the rise of many independent states in Africa and Asia. Some of this literature even contended that the goal of modernization was the creation of democratic political systems everywhere. It sketched continua to pinpoint the position of various societies and systems on the scale of modernity and democracy. The measurement was conducted with the aid of hypothesized criteria and indices, including the enumeration of functions essential to any political system that can be applied for testing purposes to any environment. Implicit in this approach was not merely the projection of the Western norm, but also the universality of human experience. Now, one can argue that denominators like industrialization, technology, and similar variables have the force of universality. But can one as easily argue the universality of beliefs, and the corollary commitments that these beliefs impose upon individuals and societies? If, for example, the belief in individual liberty and the capacity to act freely that this precept presumably affords — or the assumption of rights for individuals based on a Higher Law of Nature or Reason — are essential components of a political philosophy that moves societies to arrange a peculiar polity for their well-being, can one assume that such tenets can be readily produced in societies holding, or adhering to, different, and possibly contrary, beliefs by the reproduction of conditions which led to the rise of a particular socio-political system elsewhere and at an earlier time in history? One society's concept of man and his place in the world can lead to the pursuit of different ends despite the use of means similar to those used by a society that starts out with different concepts and premises about these matters. If objective conditions are the minimum requirement for a process of modernization, subjective commitments, which are absolutely essential, can vary.

One need not deny the hypothesized eventuality of the so-called modernization process as a universal occurrence. In fact, one can suggest that the trend of revolution in Europe since the Enlightenment and, especially in the nineteenth and twentieth centuries, has been to secularize the social and political life of man on earth. Without discussing the Rousseau formula of the 'general will' and the subsequent movements of regicide — the destruction of divine sovereign right, or any legitimate sovereignty deriving from other than human sources — or the Nietzschean 'will to power' and the Hegelian apotheosis of history, this militancy on the part of man to secularize his existence and its meaning led him via Marx to conceive of the end of history. The end was not however to usher in an afterlife, but a perfect life on earth. Regardless of the economic analyses marshalled in favour of secularization, the fact remains that such a concept and view of man in history has been made possible — though one may not think that it necessarily reflects reality — by an essentially ideological and political dogma.

One could easily imagine an extension of this revolutionary trend in Asia and Africa and, in this particular instance, in the Middle East. But whereas in Europe the revolution followed a rather fierce and prolonged conflict between religious and temporal power, this conflict never really occurred in Muslim societies. Temporal power in these societies was for centuries supported, in theory at least, by the authority of a revealed Sacred Law. The distinction between temporal and spiritual power was never argued, let alone couched, in the elaborate dicta of philosophical schemes or doctrines. One actually complemented the other. This relationship might conceivably advance the desire and capacity of the current revolution in these societies to deny all sacred history by enthroning the profane. Yet, because of it, one does not have to be distinguished from the other, and the advancement of the temporal by virtue of this relationship becomes synonymous with the advancement of the spiritual. In order to work for the power and glory of his earthly city, man in Islam does not have to kill God; for the interpretation of God's revealed message views the establishment of a powerful realm of the faithful on earth as a duty incumbent upon all believers.

If this relationship is accepted, one may argue that revolution in Islam is the struggle for status, prestige, and power, the ceaseless quest of all politics for security and advantage, irrespective of the means used to achieve these ends. Moreover, these ends can be advanced through the central position accorded to the ruler-leader by the religion and its developed tradition on the one hand, and by the particular importance of the state and its elite accorded by the secular revolution in general on the other. If man is to be weaned from an unseen divine master in order to follow and practise the maxims of the good life on earth that are 'scientifically' devised by his revolutionary leader, he must adopt a new creed which authorizes his submersion into a collective effort for the attainment of a powerful *civitas terrena*. For the revolution in Europe this may have entailed a long and fierce controversy. For the Muslim today, I submit, it is possible — theoretically at least — without the controversy.

Whereas much of the impetus for, and orientation of, the European revolution over the last 250 years was intellectual, the trend in the Middle East has been non-intellectual. Instead of the militant intellectual evolving the new doctrine of revolution and devising a strategy for the use of the masses to take power, the militant in this case has been the non-doctrinaire soldier, the ideological and revolutionary guerilla combatant, the conservative or fundamentalist religious agitator terrorist and the popular saviour. This is possible in an Islamic society because of the special relationship which the tradition provides between the leader and the masses. (Islamic universalism is apocalyptic.) That is why, contrary to the developments of the revolution in Europe, revolution in Islam does not render imperative the secularization of man's conception of history. The establishment of an Islamic realm of justice and power is already a political value inherent in the faith of the believer. It needs no new dogma to make it immanent.

If revolutions usually provide a society with greater state power, the Islamic conception of the desired society is already couched in terms of a powerful state or secular order. The latter, in turn, implies status and recognition. If recognition and status are really the ultimate ends of revolution in Islamic states today, absolute categories of political development and modernization are misleading, if not of little help. In the end, men choose between ultimate values; they choose as they do, because their life and thought are determined by fundamental moral categories and concepts that are as much a part of their being and conscious thought and sense of their own identity as their basic physical structure. Theories of political modernization so far, suggest intelligently how things are or could be done, but not *what* things ought to be done. To this extent, such theories imply the necessary triumph of a particular rational process and its peculiar blueprint for change. They tend therefore to treat most matters of politics as technical problems, yet their conclusions about them are more likely than not value-laden, despite the protestations of their authors about their innocence regarding an indulgence in and circumscription by, value judgements.

While the means to revolution in Islamic societies today and the solutions they may seek to socio-economic problems may appear similar to those adopted elsewhere, say in Europe, the ends can be different. Thus, even though some leaders in

Islamic societies have recently sought to dethrone the sacred tradition in order to 'modernize' Islamic society, their efforts did not preclude the goal of creating a new dominion of modern Muslims. This may very well have been the essence of their rebellion. The first step towards this end was the search for status and recognition, that is, independence; the next step was the absolute subordination of the individual to an authoritarian leadership which permitted the reinforcement of state power for the achievement of a strong dominion. Not only were technological and military means recruited to attain this end, but also religious and cultural ones. Institutionalized and rigidly hierarchical, religion in Europe was the enemy of the revolution and had to be excluded from the struggle for man's political 'progress' and emancipation. In some instances it had to be replaced. In Islamic societies, on the other hand, the revolution, whether for modernity or the restoration of the Islamic polity, does not face the same difficulty since religion condones and urges the political domination of the believer over earthly society.

Islam then has been a source of legitimacy for all power. All other man-made institutions were of secondary importance. Institutions and rules were therefore difficult to create. The dialectic of individual freedom versus state coercion, similarly, was never dealt with. If authority is seen to be derived from a superhuman, i.e. divine source, and power to be based upon a divine message, there is little chance of its limitation by human standards. Theoretically, it is exercised under certain religious constraints. This has been a continuous tradition since ancient Egypt and Mesopotamia, where rulers were also chief-soldiers and judges. In imposing their authority and seeking the obedience of their subjects they usually invoked sanctions in the name of a god and a panoply of other supernatural entities or constructs.

But the legacy of political authority is not one of mere scripture or religious doctrine; rather, it is a complex religio-cultural ethos, the social and economic conditions of a civilisation associated with a vast political dominion, e.g. the Ottoman state, other slave and praetorian dynasties, the impact of the West, reformism and radical integrative ideologies of recent times. Yet, on the whole, the political ideology inherited from the past is static, consecrated in orthodoxy. Its rejection has always meant subversion, rebellion, heresy and even apostasy. The idea of politics and the state has hardly been dynamic. And this perhaps is the attraction of someone like the Ayatollah Khomeini, who has overturned the old quietistic, typically Shii dissimulating attitude to power and rendered it immanentist, activist and dynamic. Nevertheless, the problem of political integration in the nation-state remains intractable, even in Khomeini's Iran, and in all states which comprise diverse ethnic, sectarian and religious communities. And it remains so under militant Islam because of its exclusiveness and restorative thrust for the realization of the true *umma*, or religious community. The fragmented social structure — in varying degrees — of Middle Eastern states, reflected and expressed in sectarian and ethnic strife, renders them, with the odd exception, firstly, anything but nation-states, and secondly, states in which Muslims live.

The difficulty in accepting the territorial aspect of nationalism and dimension of the nation-state may be illustrated by concrete cases of historical experience. When there was a dispute in 1906 between the Porte and Egypt regarding territorial sovereignty over Taba near Aqaba, Mustafa Kamil's National Party, which sought full independence for Egypt and whose mass of followers were Muslim Egyptians, was not keen to retain the territory for Egypt, preferring the integrity of the *umma* which then still had a Commander, the Ottoman Sultan and Caliph. It was the British who insisted on a territorial settlement in favour of Egypt.

Another example is the contrast between the Arabs' struggle to keep Palestine Arab in the face of the Jewish-Zionist claim. From the beginning, at least until 1967, the struggle was based on a wider cultural identity, the Arab-Islamic, whereas that of the Jews centred on territory. This explains in part the cultural perception of the protagonists. The Arabs of Palestine recognized their wider 'cultural sea' of Arab-Islam and were more readily willing in 1945–8 to retreat into that familiar sea.

Furthermore, the desperate search by non-Muslim Arabs for a more secular, less religious-based, nationalism to obviate their minority status is manifested in their leadership of so many blatantly secular nationalist movements, ranging from Arab nationalism to a Greater Syrian nationalism (Antoun Saadeh), local Lebanese or Egyptian nationalism, all of which combined territory with historical, economic and ethnic variables and varieties of Marxism and Communism.

There are also paradoxes in the questions of territory and religious identity regarding states. By the 1930s several rulers in the Middle East — Abdullah, Faisal, Ibn Saud — discovered that internationally recognized boundaries were the best guarantee for the identity and integrity of their respective states. This could well be a function of the proverbial and perennial irredentist claims and counterclaims between them, in a region where boundaries are recent artificial creations of foreign power fiat, or simply remain undemarcated. But no case can be made for any of these states, or the smaller Gulf emirates, being nation-states. A follower of Karl Deutsch would argue that with the further development of communications and economic institutions this may yet come to pass. But who is to say?

The state, expressing a dynast's, satrap's or despot's power, nevertheless seems to be the most durable political structure for the organization of power in Islam. But even that is being challenged today: its structures and the legitimacy of its rulers are under attack from the Levant to southwest Asia. Thus domestic conflict and its corollary of regional instability threatens the further balkanization of the region and therefore the redrawing of its map. The latter has already occurred in Palestine and Lebanon; it could ensue from the Iran-Iraq war, as well as from events in South Arabia and North Africa. It is being accompanied by an Islamic revolution which suggests that obedience, or political obligation, need no longer be, as it has been for the past 1,000 years, unconditional. Militant political Islam is now a threat to existing regimes, and one cannot say to what extent Muslim rulers of Muslim states can control and contain political Islam.

Militant Islam today may constitute a threat to existing regimes in the Middle East and to the very existence of the state, even if, as I have tried to show, it is not quite a nation-state. It is not certain, however, that it also constitutes an international political movement with specific goals. For the moment a number of leaders, or rulers, have used it as a device by which they, as weak states, make demands on the more powerful ones. Within the region, however, it may well be designed to redistribute power, influence and wealth. To the extent that, as in the recent case of Iran, or the opportunities afforded by the combination of petro-wealth and access to the means of violence, it rejects the present world order with its international customs and conventions, the question arises of how well it can be coped with? Can a world order, based on such secular notions as interest, balance of power, competition and compromise in the conduct of relations between states, deal with one based on the conflict of religio-cultural and civilizational values? If the militant Islamic movement rejects the nation-state in favour of the *umma*, its interference in the internal affairs of other states is — theoretically, at least — viewed as legitimate. And this is a problem.

There are those of course who argue that the nation-state is on its way out; it is no longer as important or useful, and they point to the EEC in northwestern Europe. Yet states have proliferated since 1945, provided we accept the fact that most of them are not nation-states but what some have called imitation states. The state remains the main actor on the political stage. But it too, if terrorism is a criterion, has its problems.

The question really is whether a state inhabited and governed by Muslims can ever be a purely secular one, the *sine qua non* of a nation-state. The answer for the moment is that it cannot. The concept of toleration (*aman* and *dhimma*) suggests that is the case, and mainly because a Muslim must not share power with a non-Muslim. He can share economic goods, social benefits and space, but not power.

In a 1986 interview with the London *Sunday Times*, Muhammad Hasanein Heikal, Chief Editor of *al-Ahram* from 1957 to 1974 and President Nasser's confidant, suggested that President Sadat was assassinated because he became too closely associated and identified with the United States and the West. I say that in the minds of the Muslim militants who killed him he was identified with alien, infidel ideas and forces. In fact, he was assassinated specifically because he had treated harshly their leaders and fellow militants. Twenty-four years earlier the Egyptian Premier, Nuqrashi, was assassinated by the Secret Organization of the Muslim Brotherhood for precisely the same reason: he had just dissolved and proscribed their organization, and arrested many of its leaders. Indeed, any ruler who maintains the secular features of the state is considered by these groups as heretic, an apostate and an infidel; his elimination by force (or his liquidation) is therefore permitted. The game of power is also very much in the forefront. The attempt by the Muslim Brotherhood on Nasser's life in 1954 ḧatever the assumed connivance of the Free Officers may have been, was the direct consequence of his having denied them a share in power.

Rulers of Middle Eastern states have for over a century now relentlessly eroded the religious character of the state. The expansion of state functions has been purely at the expense of the role of certain religious leaders and institutions. At the same time, alas, they have failed to provide an acceptable alternative basis for the legitimacy of the state and its patterns of authority, including one centred on the imported doctrine of nationalism with its structure of the nation-state. While the non-Muslim subjects of these states sought a political answer to their problem in secular integrative ideologies, the body politic remained fragmented. Modernity in the meantime produced further and sharper dichotomies, a divorce from Islamic sources of authority without integration on a new basis. A duality of power arising from the duality of the sources of legitimacy and legislation has prevailed — always uncomfortable and precarious. It is this failure which is now being held up by the militant Muslims as evidence for the cogency of their demand for a return to the Islamic polity. It is, in short, a bid for power on the heels of the failure of radical nationalists and so-called socialists, modernizing soldier-despots and petro-rich dynastic rulers. A bid for power does not mean necessarily the reinstatement of the idealized *umma*, let alone its reconstitution. As the Iranian episode has amply demonstrated, it can mean simply the exclusive control of the *state* — and I emphasize the state, that enduring power structure in Islam — by those who purport to reject what are perceived to be alien and hostile notions and institutions in favour of indigenous Islamic ones. Whether one has in mind Zia ul Haq in Pakistan, Khomeini in Iran or Kadhafi in Libya, the pattern is the same. If the earliest crises of legitimacy in Islam were dealt with by force — civil war — subsequent ones, including those of today, may well be met but not solved in the same way.

A condition of stasis exists throughout the Middle East, generated by the recurring clash between tradition and modernity, and the challenge of the latter by the native Muslim ethic, from Turkey to the Sudan and from Pakistan to Morocco. This puts in question the whole range of social, economic and political development in the region since 1920, if not before. It also reintroduces an old dichotomy, nay antagonism, between things Islamic and non-Islamic, or Muslim versus non-Muslim. The antagonism may never be resolved, but its course will most probably be settled by force, i.e. by those who can control the state structure of power. Unless, of course, Muslims somehow resolve their central problem of the relation between power and faith, or between religion and public order. It is not incidentally a matter that outsiders can settle, or even help to resolve.

The question of Islam and political power, or Islam and the state, is a recurrent phenomenon. Today, the basic feature of states in the Middle East (perhaps exceptions are arguable) is the 'fortress regime', a phrase coined by my friend the Swiss scholar and journalist Dr Arnold Hottinger, where an individual or group — military, ethnic, sectarian, or partisan — once in control of central power fights off the periodic attacks or threats of the disaffected and challenging peripheries.

3

The Return of Islam to Politics or Radical Islam: Promise and Reality

Ever since the tenth–eleventh centuries (with the exception of the Ismaili Fatimid state in Egypt) Islam has been divorced from state politics, from the arrangements and exercise of state power. Its revealed Sacred Law, the *sharia*, has been confined to the regulation of personal status and social matters. Rulers — caliphs, sultans, minor local dynasts, despots and satraps — legitimized their authority in the eyes of the faithful by allowing religious teachers and jurisconsults free rein to guide and adjudicate the private life of the believers in the community and the social order. They also legitimized it by defending the community of the faithful against external — infidel — threats and attacks. Otherwise, their authority rested on their secular power — the sword — and they governed, albeit theoretically, whenever and wherever possible within the purview of the religious law, mainly by decree, ordinance and plain dispensation, often in flagrant violation of the Sacred Law.

Until the beginning of the nineteenth century, Sunni jurists and religious teachers accepted and rationalized this separation of central power and Islamic society, of power and sanctity. Indeed, they realized that only the Prophet Muhammad could combine the two functions. Even the immediate successors to this temporal authority over the community of Muslims could not lay claim to the prophetic function; only to the temporal leadership and spiritual preceptorship of the faithful.

Unable seriously to influence power, the jurists contented themselves with the privileged position offered them by the ruler or dynast as guardians of the word of God, as teachers, scholars and judges. Soon they accepted the separation between sanctity and power. Having produced their massive legal compendia according to their interpretation of the Koran, *sunna* (life, conduct) and *hadith* (sayings) of the Prophet, they formulated the proposition that obedience to the ruler, good or bad, pious or sinner, was better than *fitna* (anarchy, disorder). In other words, they legitimized the status quo. This was tantamount to the formal consecration of political quietism in Islam.

As for the presumed supremacy of the Sacred Law, the jurists conveniently proclaimed it an ideal standard for Muslim life and conduct; but it was to remain an ideal in this erring and sinful world until the coming of the expected *mahdi* (the divinely guided saviour), who would apply it in its entirety and establish an order of righteousness and justice. This was a typical medieval compromise between the real (earthly power) and the ideal, allowing for a symbiotic coexistence between the separate realm of state power and that of the Sacred Law. It was a situation that prevailed throughout Islamic history.

Such a comfortable, albeit stagnant, rigid, subservient and ambivalent-ambiguous position of Islam *vis-à-vis* the state did not really matter very much so long as the dominion of Islam and its territory was governed by a Muslim ruler or rulers who could defend it against its non-Muslim enemies. When, however, in the late eighteenth–early nineteenth century an economically, militarily and technologically superior Europe began to threaten and encroach upon the lands of Islam, the decline and eventual defeat of the last great Muslim empire, the Ottoman, became a real possibility.

Neither the Islamic political order nor its religious establishment appeared able to deal with this modern infidel threat. Ever since that time, coping with modernity of infidel provenance became one of the most vexing problems of Islamic rulers and communities. It was compounded, moreover, by a deep psychological trauma when Muslims discovered that the most perfect religion — which had been victorious on the battlefield for centuries, allowing its followers to carry on their Muslim lives undisturbed by and *uninterested in the doings of the infidels* — was now unable to stem this new infidel tide. In the past, they had defeated the Byzantines and the Persians (Sassanids) in the east, conquered Spain, Sicily and the Balkans, and reached the gates of Vienna in the heart of central Europe in the west. Suddenly, the thirteenth–fourteenth Muslim centuries became the worst in their history. During this time they succumbed to direct or indirect infidel rule, control and subservience. And this now became the most profound crisis (*miḥna*) to face Islam in its annals and historical experience.

Resist they did: the Mamluks in Egypt against Napoleon in 1798 and the native Egyptians against the British in 1882; Abdel Qadez in North Africa against the French in the 1830s; the Mahdi in the Sudan against the Anglo-Egyptian onslaught in the late 1880s and early 1890s; and the Turks against the Russians for nearly a century. But to no avail. Even where they succeeded in escaping actual European control they were forced to introduce Europeans and European ways for the more efficient conduct of public affairs. Modern armies modelled on European military organization, training, technology and weaponry replaced the more traditional corps of warriors and praetorian guards. Secular state schools teaching the subjects of modern science, foreign languages and the humanities were opened alongside the traditional ones run by the religious institutions. A new class of European-educated and trained high state officials emerged to replace the more traditional groups in serving the ruler and assisting him to govern. New laws, courts and constitutions modelled on European legal, judicial and political systems were promulgated. Economic and diplomatic relations with Europe were extended and strengthened, bringing with them new cultural and political ideas and institutions to be emulated and adopted, and requiring more secular arrangements, social behaviour and even new attitudes and perceptions.

Islam, or at least its guardians and interpreters, seemed helpless and immobilized in the face of this alien secular onslaught. Muslim reformers arose, desperately trying both to prove Islam's superiority and to reconcile its teachings with modernity — an impossible task. Insisting on Islam's superior tradition, they failed to bridge the gap and ended up as apologists for it. As a result, by 1900 the new secular 'bourgeoisie' of state officials, landowners, merchants and soldiers had won the leadership contest. The stronger central government became and the more effective state control over the country and society, the weaker the traditional conservative groups of religion found themselves. They gradually lost their central role even as arbiters of personal Muslim conduct and the social order. Soon they were no more than salaried servants of the new secular state.

Whereas Muslim reformers who tried to modernize Islam

failed, they succeeded in a different way in areas untouched by the European virus. The Wahhabis in Arabia in the late eighteenth century for example, using the authority of certain medieval theologians, established a virulent movement of purified — and puritanical — Islam, based strictly on the teachings of the Koran and the *sunna* of the Prophet, free of centuries-old accretions. The movement, however, remained confined to the Arabian Peninsula and particularly to Najd. Yet the house of Saud, in alliance with the Wahhabis, carved a kingdom in the twentieth century which, until the discovery of oil, resisted all infidel encroachments and temptations.

Elsewhere in the Middle East, though, Islam was in retreat, overwhelmed by the combination of European control and local secular state development. With the destruction of the Ottoman empire in 1918, several successor states very much reflected this trend. Liberal constitutional and parliamentary political experiments in Egypt and the Fertile Crescent were soon accompanied by ideological movements of secular state nationalism, Arabism and, later, socialism. Rulers and governments paid lip service to Islam, especially those among them who needed to legitimize their authority in the eyes of the overwhelming mass of their Muslim subjects, or to oppose other Muslim rulers and governments. Their secular arrangements for state power were understood and looked after by a very small elite of 'modern' men. They did not excite or elicit the understanding, let alone loyalty, of the vast public whose members continued to lead their lives on the basis of traditional-religious values and to view the world with traditional perceptions under the guidance and with the advice of their religious teachers. The rulers and the new secular elite, on the other hand, simply bypassed or ignored the question of religion. To be sure they paid formal obeisance by making it the official religion of the state, or by conceding to it periodically, under pressure and for political reasons, a formal primacy as a source of legislation. But they never really either determined its position in, and relation to, the state, or tried to make their new secular state creed acceptable to its adherents.

The ambivalence and laxity of the secular state authorities and the new secular intelligentsia undermined secularism itself. The moment that European control retreated from the lands of Islam and European influence diminished, secularism declined and its appeal evaporated. The subsequent failure of its representatives and advocates — state nationalists, Arab nationalists and socialists — to defend the Islamic nation, the community of the faithful in the mid- and late twentieth century against a new alien infidel enemy, Israel, eroded their position further and encouraged more traditional Islamic forces to question its relevance and challenge the authority of its supporters and purveyors. Thus, in the period from the 1930s to the 1950s the Muslim Brotherhood (Society of Muslim Brothers), founded by a sufi elementary school teacher, Hasan el Banna, as a charitable religious society in 1928, became the largest mass Islamic religio-political movement on any reckoning in modern times. Its involvement in Egyptian politics and, wider afield, in the politics of neighbouring Arab states by the Second World War was so intensive as to pose a serious threat to the security of successive Egyptian regimes, including that of the soldiers under Nasser after 1952. More effectively autocratic, the latter finally proscribed and dissolved the Brotherhood, executed its leaders, and interned and persecuted thousands of its members and sympathizers.

Unlike the old 'modernizing' Muslim reformers earlier in this century and before, the Muslim Brotherhood put forward a more radical revolutionary programme, not to reform Islam, but to return to the basic teachings of its Fathers and, by violent means if necessary, to make it the exclusive basis of rule and the political order. In short, they proposed an alternative socio-political order to the existing one.[1] Internment, torture and persecution, however, took their toll, and forced the old leadership of the Brotherhood to make compromises with Caesar or Pharaoh, the secular state. Equally, though, these trials and tribulations spawned a new ideological and organizational development within its ranks that was far more radical and uncompromising in its characterization of present-day Islamic society, state and rule as un-Islamic and infidel (*jahiliyya*), to be fought relentlessly and destroyed, and to be replaced by a purely Islamic order.

These new offshoots of the Brotherhood rejected the long-standing separation of sanctity and power, Islamic society and the state, the old political quietism of conservative traditional religious teachers who had obsequiously succumbed to secular state authority. Islam and Muslims, according to these new puritans and 'Calvinists' among the faithful, had to be brought back to the centre of politics with a view to establishing an

Islamic dominion once again, free of alien infidel and other non-Islamic encumbrances. Moreover, the apostles and followers of this new creed of radical Islam were to reject the polluted society around them as corrupt and un-Islamic. They were to form a counter-society that would lead the movement for the return to true Islam, undiluted and unpolluted by the virus of infidel modernity. These are the new Radical Sunni Muslims, whose organizations are to be found in Egypt, Syria, Lebanon and elsewhere in the Arab Muslim world.[2]

The trials and tribulations of the Muslim Brotherhood at the hands of the authorities from 1954 to 1966 culminated in the execution of Sayyid Qutb, the first major ideologue of Radical Islam. It may be said that the new Radical Muslim societies were born in the crucible of state persecution. Armed already with a fairly comprehensive ideology provided by Qutb[3] they were able to elaborate its varied organizational applications and programmes of revolutionary action. Some of their leaders, like Shukri Mustafa and Abdel Salam Farag, to mention only two, built further on the 'master's' (Qutb's) writings by adding their own interpretative gloss and refining their own political-ideological platforms into a plan of action.

The seditious and violent activities of these new groups in the period 1974–81 ranged from the bloody attack on the Cairo Military Technical College, the abduction and murder of a Minister of Waqfs and clashes with the army and police in Middle and Upper Egypt, to the assassination of Sadat. It was a manifestation of the return of Islam to the centre of politics, as the guide to political action. Such actions highlighted the confrontation between militant Islam and the secular state, between 'sanctity' and power, between Prophet and Pharaoh — as Gilles Keppel put it dramatically in his book, *Muslim Extremism in Egypt*.

Significantly, these new militant groups and their activities represented the break between the new Radical Islamic groups and the older mother organization, the Muslim Brotherhood. This reflected the differences between the older, more 'staid' remnants of the Brotherhood establishment, gathered in the 1970s around the publications *Da'wa* and *I'tisam*, on the one hand, and the new militants on the other.

There is however yet a third type of advocate of the return to Islam, one who is more at home with modern electronic media — TV and cassette — but who does not particularly share the militants' option for violence. Such are the notorious popular preachers Sheikhs Abdel Hamid Kishk, Ahmad Mahallawi and Muhammad Mitwalli Sah'rawi in Egypt. Kishk has been what Kepel called, quoting a Saudi-funded magazine, 'the star of Islamic preaching'. His audiences extend to North Africa and Muslim communities in southern France.

When the radical Islamic movement took over university student unions in the late seventies many of its leaders were either well-versed in other ideologies, particularly Marxism, or were lapsed Marxists themselves. But one must not conclude that the Islamic movement is infiltrated by Communists. Rather the movement succeeded in the 1970s in becoming an effective mode of expressing social protest; that is, an acceptable form of political discourse. But it is one of several ways of resisting deprivation, oppression and disorientation. There are, that is, still other outlets available to Egyptians, such as popular ridicule of authority, lethargy and inertia in carrying out its orders — sabotage by inaction — avoiding contact with state authority by seeking a livelihood in the private sector, or simply escaping the intolerable conditions of life at home by leaving the country. In short, there are still Egyptians who are very reluctant to return to the centre of political action, even on the back of militant Islam. To this extent, a sociological explanation of the phenomenon of militant Islam is extremely limited, inadequate and, in the final analysis, irrelevant.

Perhaps the most lasting effect of militant Islam on the new generation of Egyptians over the past twenty years is, as Kepel contends, to have made the proverbial dialectic of daily Egyptian private and public life of *ma'lesh* ('it does not matter') and *bakhshish* (bribery) unacceptable to them. A more serious and profound conclusion here is Sivan's, regarding the seizing by militant Islam of 'cultural hegemony' in Egypt.[4]

The 'utopia' first envisaged by Qutb, and subsequently attempted by Shukri Mustafa and others, suggests that the militants underestimated the resilience of the state in repulsing their attacks. Their inability to take on the state directly led them to attack other targets, in particular the Christian minority — the Coptic community first — and subsequently to 'cut down the Pharaoh himself'.

That there is a confrontation between Prophet and Pharaoh in countries like Egypt is certain; it is a very old confrontation. But that Prophet is about to attain earthly power is not so certain. Egyptianism (state territorial nationalism: Pharaoh) will remain pitted against Arabo-Islamism (Prophet) for a long time to come. Even if Prophet attained power he would have to transform himself into Pharaoh in order to govern and survive.[5]

Although the possibility of militant Muslim societies acceding to state power in, say, Egypt, is remote, one must still reckon with their potential recruitment opportunities from a vast sea of the plainly traditional faithful, what Professor Sivan called the 'conservative periphery of radicalism', especially at a time when the latter's return to Islam since 1967 has been massive.

Intellectually interesting is the way radical Muslims have constructed an ideology for Sunni rebellion against authority. Bearing in mind the centuries-old tradition of political quietism this process is crucial. Sayyid Qutb, the ideologue of the radical wing of the Muslim Brotherhood who was executed by the Nasser regime in 1966, had a central role in this process. It was he who supplied the ideological-theoretical justification for Sunni revolt against authority. Influenced by the Indian–Pakistani divine Abu al-A'la' al-Mawdudi and his disciple Abu al-Hasan al-Nadvi, Qutb developed his concept of the *jahiliyya*: barbaric, un-Islamic) society, where the dominion of man over man instead of that of God prevails.[6] Grounding his argument further on the thought of the medieval theologian–philosopher Ibn Taymiyya, Qutb was able to formulate a straightforward theory of Sunni revolution. Ibn Taymiyya had developed a theory of the right of resistance to illegitimate rulers who do not apply a substantial part of the *sharia*, such as the Muslim Mongols of his time. His thought was one of the bases of the Wahhabi revivalist puritanical movement in eighteenth-century Arabia.[7]

Qutb worked out an elaborate three-party theory of resistance to tyrannical — un-Islamic — rule. He diagnosed the ill of contemporary Islamic society as being *modernity*, in which the laws and the dominion of man have replaced those of God. Its chief characteristic is secularism: the modern interventionist state which wholly controls civil society with its new idols of economic growth and development as these are articulated via nationalism, Arabism and socialism. It is aided and abetted by the official religious establishment that has succumbed to control by the infidel state. Both therefore are infidel and must be fought. Secondly, the only cure for this ill is *rebellion*, spearheaded by the vanguard of true believers (the counter-society referred to earlier, what Sivan called the 'Republic of the Virtuous'[8]). Thirdly, the rebellion becomes the *jihad* (holy war) which entails sacrifice and martyrdom for the sake of the community.

This basic Qutb formulation was further developed, altered and, in certain cases, radicalized — if that is possible — by his disciples Shukri Mustafa of the Muslim Society (more popularly known as *Takfir wa Higra*), Abdel Salam Farag of the Jihad (members of this group assassinated President Sadat of Egypt on 6 October 1981), Salih Sirriya and others. The point about these younger disciples of Qutb is that they were all urban-centred and university graduates in science and engineering.

Cultural pessimism among teachers of Islam, Muslim reformers and more lay traditional Muslims in general has been pervasive for at least 200 years now, if not longer. The new generation of Radical Muslims are equally pessimistic about the condition of Islam and Muslim society, but combine their pessimism with a radical revolutionary activism that rejects the secular state and social order of the last 200 years as barbaric and infidel (some of them even reject all legislation after the foundation of the Umayyad Caliphate in Damascus in 660 AD, or consider it as suspect at least) and their leaders and rulers as usurpers. They abhor equally the Left which assisted in the expansion of secular state power, thus undermining the autonomy of civil society where at least Islam operated until the nineteenth century. They then proceed to outline how they will establish their own alternative order.

A most important step in this direction is the call by the Radicals for authenticity, the rejection of modernity, of modernist apologetic Islam and *the return of Islam itself to active politics*. They reject imported political ideas such as popular sovereignty and majority rule (not different really from the first generation of Brotherhood leaders like Abdel Qadir Auda and others in the forties and fifties who also rejected these ideas).[9] For them Islam is not and never was democratic. All those who follow man-made laws are infidel and must be fought. Nationalists are to be opposed too because they limit the territorial expression and extension of Radical Islam. For the moment, the Radicals must shun the *jahili* society by 'emigrating' from it to form a counter-society, the model for the society of the future; must prepare themselves by education and prayer; and, when ready, must violently overthrow the usurpers in preparation for reform.

The old jurists' preference for order over *fitna* (anarchy or disorder) must be abandoned in order to uproot infidelity. *Jihad*, which one of the Radical ideologues called the 'Absent Precept' or the 'Hidden Imperative' (*al-farida al-gha'iba*), is of the essence in this process. Since man is the agent of God in accomplishing His will, he must reject quietism and aloofness from politics. So long as the powerful modern state impinges upon social life, the old quietistic passive tradition of the majority of Sunni Muslims who compromised with it is no longer valid. Only the seizure of power by the virtuous Muslims can guarantee the survival of Islam. Indeed, in the view of Radical Muslims the situation today is similar(!) to that in the period when the first Caliph Abu Bakr had to fight the apostate tribes in the Wars of Ridda (Wars of Apostasy).

What the Radical Muslims have subtly introduced into Islamic political discourse is a contractual theory of government which makes dissidence and rebellion possible. At the same time they reject the appurtenances of such recent policies as the Open Door economic policy in Egypt, economic growth and development which bring along consumerism, the modern idols of selfishness and ill-gotten wealth, rising expectations, laxity in sexual mores, the dissolution of the family, electronic media and an influx of infidel foreigners; in short, the materialism of modern science and technology and ever greater secularism.

The impact of the trauma suffered by this new generation of Radical Muslims as a result of persecution and imprisonment cannot be overestimated. It is reflected in their more blunt treatment of the question of non-Muslims if the *sharia* were to be strictly applied — a course they advocate — and their fundamentalist insistence that the transcendental is not subject to the scrutiny of reason. In trying to counter the new Radicals the authorities mobilize the official religious establishment to show in debate, writing and preaching that the Radicals are really outside the consensus (*ijma*ʿ) of the Sunni community; that they are 'the Kharijites of the twentieth century'. In this connection, one must point to the rather clever and fairly successful measures taken by President Mubarak's regime in Egypt after the assassination of his predecessor, in order to erode the appeal of the Radicals. Through a combination of good security measures, periodically lenient treatment of lesser members of Radical Muslim organizations and a freer press that allows other opposition groups to express their views — i.e. an alternative opposition to Radical Islam — Mubarak yanked out the fangs of the movement.

However, the real threat of the Radical Muslims — to public order — remains. In view of the weakness, not to mention repeated failure of the Arab Left and other secular intellectuals there is tremendous scope for further gains by Radical Islam. The Left not only failed to make secularism an acceptable ideology of the masses, but also fatally overlooked the 'deep anchor' of Islam for the life of the masses and significantly that of the educated youth. Several empirical surveys of the 1960s, 1970s and 1980s found Islam to be a major component of 'secular' Arabism and a very resilient component of identity, individual and communal existence. The Left also failed to discuss the question of minorities or to deal with the impact of the civil war in Lebanon. As regards the latter, the Radical Muslims argue that, as a product of Christian culture, secularism cannot easily be transplanted to a region shaped by Islam: confessionalism in Lebanon is deep-rooted and indigenous, based on that country's history and culture; it is not a French invention.

Some leftists accept the bankruptcy of their secular intellectual efforts and are prepared to make peace and cooperate with, in order to exploit, the Radical Muslims, for these are now the leading social factor in their region. Through this accommodation, they argue — unrealistically one would think — the Left can lead the masses who are Muslims and whose Islam constitutes an 'oriental specificity'; that is, the bulwark against cultural conquest by the West. In due course, the Left would transform 'Islam as the state religion' into a revolutionary ideology; that is, secularize it! If the vanguard of this phantasmagoric movement happens to be Pan-Arab, the masses — the followers — are Muslim. Islam can become the vehicle for the re-entry of the masses into politics; and it does not have to be reactionary. It can even use the mythically potent, but by now worn-out, weapon of 'Islam and Oil'. For the present, at least, these leftists consider Islam to be the sole available agent of radical change. Such convoluted thinking, however, remains a knee-jerk reaction, for the primary and ultimate objective of the Left is to oppose the West.

It is the performance of the Left after the failure of Nasser's and the Baath's radical, revolutionary Arabism which underlines its failure too. After the debacles of the period from 1961 to 1967, the masses flocked back to Islam. The post-1952 Arab Left did not even exhibit the courage of the old liberal humanists of the inter-war period — men like Taha Hussein, Ismail Mazhar, Shibli Shumayyil, Salama Musa and Ali Abdel Raziq — in trying to remove Islam from the affairs of state.[10] In 1950 only a 'younger' Azharite, Khalid Muhammad Khalid, dared to tackle the problem; and after 1967 only the Syrian secular philosopher, Sadiq Jalal al-Azm, produced a straightforward rejection of the efficacy of religion as a way for the future.[11] Nor did the Left ever meet head-on the question of Islam's role in state legislation; that is, the wider issue of the application of the *sharia*, or the more delicate one of Islam's position *vis-à-vis* non-Muslim Arab and non-Arab minorities.

Muslim Arab intellectuals generally, including those of the Left, failed to remind their audiences that secularism in politics was the order of the day in post-Muhammad or post-prophetic Islamic history, contrary to the myths of Islamic historiography — a point I emphasized in my introduction to this piece. Rule was mainly by decree; it was given *ex post facto* religious sanction by the jurists. The *sharia* was applied only to personal matters and certain commercial transactions, but not to state institutions, the transfer of power, the relations between ruler and subject, or external relations. The popular perceptions of the more mythical version of Islamic history however are deeply entrenched among the masses. An even more glaring omission by intellectuals is the fact that they have not capitalized on the tenacity of the nation-state which for several decades now has been the legitimate foundation of political life and group identity despite its contribution to centrifugal tendencies in the Muslim Arab world.

It is not of course quite clear whether in practice Radical Muslims grudgingly accept the nation-state as their operational framework. The evidence is that they do, despite the fact that their ideologues — from the old Brotherhood leadership and Qutb to the most recent — reject nationalism and the nation-state as imported Western political concepts. If Radical Islam is to replace the particularism of the nation-state and the regionalism of Pan-Arabism as a focus of supranational identity, one may imagine that this will enhance confessional cleavages as is already evident in Egypt, the Sudan, Syria, Iraq, Lebanon and Algeria. But it would also preclude receptivity to modern culture, because Islamic society is not to be polluted by 'imported thought'. There would be a new essentialism in the 'authentic and immutable character of Islamic society'.[12] It would, moreover, prevent rational choices, while in the meantime 'disenchantment with all ideologies' would lead to 'alienation bordering on nihilism'. Nor can one be too sanguine about the ability of Radical Muslims to replace the 'values of modernity by authentic Islamic ones'.[13]

One must conclude that the reality of Radical Islam is fairly gloomy. While cultural hegemony has been seized by Radical Islam, the 'bedrock of traditionalism', the 'conservative periphery', has withstood the challenge of two centuries of Westernization. It is on this that Radicalism today is founded even though Radical Muslims rebel against it. In other words, there has been more continuity than change. This bedrock, moreover, consists primarily of human fundamentals, such as the average and educated Muslim's attitudes toward life and death, sex and politics.[14] Thus the bastion of traditional Islamic values remains the family; it is the principal intermediary between the individual and his social-cultural milieu. Such values as authoritarianism, respect for seniority, male dominance, overdependence on social milieu and status, helplessness *vis-à-vis* state power and lack of personal initiative are still widely, overwhelmingly prevalent.[15]

If the Radical Muslims are the New Right they share with the Old Right a gloomy view of modern civilization in decadence. But they depart from common Sunni political theory and practice in the twentieth century: they want to take the initiative to stem further decadence by rebelling against their infidel, i.e. modernized Muslim rulers. Unlike the Left, they have also succeeded in developing an activist political philosophy for structural change while maintaining their traditional attitudes to attract the masses and turn them into firebrand revolutionaries. They have constructed a 'revolutionary mystique' of *jihad* and sacrifice for the sake of the community of the faithful.

An ominous picture and prospect indeed. Like Catholicism and Calvinism at one time in European history, Radical Islam, which may indeed raise and purify the spiritual level of Muslims, may also easily discourage free intellectual venture which very much depends on reason and imagination. It may push Muslim society back to the bondage of collective religious tradition whose benefits are confined to the select few. It will definitely kill human curiosity, the harbinger of new knowledge.

And the *umma* may well perish. Radical Islam, however noble its intentions, can — by its inflexible conceptions of piety, justice and truth — lead to cruel repression. Men giving free rein to their reason will be branded satans, their rights and humanity denied. In discussing 150 years ago the Spanish Inquisition, William Prescott concluded: 'Many a bloody page of history attests the fact, that fanaticism armed with power is the secret evil which can befall a nation'.[16]

If Arabism and secularism have failed to provide the basis of social protest against a system viewed to be ailing, so has Islam as a social force over several centuries. In this connection, the best writing to come from a Muslim intellectual in the last two years are two books referred to earlier, by Egyptian Ambassador Husein Ahmad Amin, *Dalil al-muslim al-Ḥazin* (The Guide of the Sad Muslim) and *Ḥawla al-daʿwa ila tatbiq al-shariʿa* (Concerning the Call or Movement to Apply the *Sharia*). In these two extraordinary books, Amin points to the dismal ignorance of Islamic texts and history by both Radical Muslims and the more traditional religious teachers. Courageously, clearly, eruditely and analytically, he suggests to both groups that there is no golden path to earthly salvation; that one can defend both Islam, the religious tradition, *and* the toleration needed to accommodate man's interests in this world. Belief, he insists, must be emancipated from dogma.

4

Islam and Nationalism: The Problem of Secularism

Back in the mid-1960s, some of us argued against the tendency of Western students to give an ideological interpretation of politics in the Arab states. We were accused of cynicism, and these students went on describing and interpreting Arab nationalism, Arab socialism and military *coups d'état* in ideological terms. They constructed a whole new political vocabulary in dealing with that part of the world, including terms like revolution, reaction, progressive and conservative, militant and moderate. Unfortunately, neither the new vocabulary nor the ideological interpretation of events and developments in the Arab states helped us understand the reality of politics and political behaviour in those societies. Nor did the enthusiasm for new trends and ideas that Western students assumed had seized the Arab 'political mind' explain the tremendous difficulties all of these states have faced since independence. In our plea that we temper our ideological interpretation with an historical-social examination of the environment, the context of politics in these states was emphasized. In other words, some of us had suggested that we ask the question, 'What kind of political experience did these societies have so far?' By doing this, some of us argued, we could identify and enumerate the social basis of and the economic and other constraints on their political behaviour that seemed often to ignore — at times transcend and transgress — their expressed ideology and their proclaimed political objectives. But no one listened to these pleas and suggestions. The Foundations were pouring money into what they were doing.

Leaving the methodological argument aside, the problem of, say, Arab nationalism and its decline in the last decade or two, is directly related to the obstacles and constraints it met in Arab societies. It is elementary to suggest that the first obstacle was the fact that nationalism as an ideology came from outside the Middle East, a region in which the majority of its inhabitants already possessed a political ideology of their own, Islam. Nationalism, an alien political ideology, was adopted by some indigenous political elites in order to avoid domestic tension and civil strife and to withstand the pressure of external threats and influence.[1] But in order to survive at all, this new imported ideology had to be wedded to the indigenous, or native, political ideology of Islam. Thus its adoption and spread were not uniform. It was, for instance, more widespread among the Arabs of the Fertile Crescent and/or the Levant, less so in the Nile Valley, rather slow and late in the Maghreb where foreign European control was tight and more direct, and non-existent in the Arabian Peninsula where it was hardly needed as a basis or a prop for political identity. But where it was needed most (as in the Fertile Crescent) it had to be radical for at least two reasons. One was the need to cope with fragmented ethnic and sectarian societies and the desire to integrate them into nation-states; the other was the need to overcome the territorial fragmentation imposed by outside powers over a people that considered itself Arab and, in the majority, Muslim.

By 1920 the concept of the nation-state came to define the state in terms of territory, language, descent, common national identity and political loyalty. In the Fertile Crescent (Iraq and Syria) the new state had to be radically nationalist, i.e. pan-Arab, because the states created by foreign powers there were not coterminous with the nation.

Another shattering illusion came with the nation-state. According to the ideology of nationalism, a nation governs itself. The Arabs acquired several nation-states but did not govern themselves for a long time (e.g. during the mandates). An early aim of radical nationalism, therefore, was the attainment of self-rule ('complete independence' in populist parlance). Soon the assumption that nationalism does away with despotism (alien or native) flowing from the premise that nation-states are self-governing, was proved false. Finally, there was the intellectual fiction created by nationalism. In the pre-nationalist past, one was a Muslim, a Cairene, a Damascene, a Beiruti, or a Baghdadi; with state nationalism one soon became an Egyptian, a Syrian, a Lebanese, an Iraqi.

But when nationalism was linked to Islam, it failed to accommodate the different, or other, the non-Muslims, and thus accelerated the inappropriateness and the decline of non-Islamic nationalism as an acceptable political ideology.

In the case of Arab nationalism there was an even greater obstacle to its being accepted, or imposed, as the only, or uniform, political ideology for Arabs. Not only was it alien and secular in origin, but it required a personal and societal commitment to a political philosophy with a secular political culture, one that abandoned dogma in favour of toleration of opposing views, one that accepted experimentation, and one that removed authority, power and the law from their divine provenance and/or link. Furthermore, it required the generation of a 'public ethic' to which most members of society subscribed — a new kind of civil consensus. This, in turn, meant closing the gap between the most durable organization for power in Middle Eastern history and Islamic annals, the state and society, or the state and public order. And for that, one needed a basically corporate society, a people organized as a public. It is difficult historically to overlook these problems, which came home to roost, so to speak, in this century. When in 1969–70 I complained about the political aridity of Arab nationalism, radical or otherwise, I suggested that,

> Radical change has occurred largely in the area of the economic activities and aspirations of Middle Eastern states: it is the result of a fantastic oil industry, improved communications, the massive infusion of arms into the region by external powers, and the extensive economic and technical aid received from them. Yet the ambivalence of the Middle Easterners regarding an organizing principle of political and social life essentially continues as one between an ethos inherited from the cultural and political experience under varieties of Islamic domination on the one hand, and several imported varieties on the other.[2]

Now, nearly 20 years later, every member of the so-called Arab intelligentsia echoes this sentiment, or borrows this assessment; although at the time it was made, Englishmen accused its author of being anti-Arab![3]

In assessing Arab nationalism one cannot avoid a consideration of the concept of the state and its nature in the Arab world.

It is linked to the conception of nationhood that each of these states adopts in order to legitimize its existence. It is also linked to the concept of nation and nationalism as referring to both individual states and the wider pan-Arab framework. Similarly, it is related to the concept of national and regional integration on the basis of the limited Arab experience. It is for this reason that I submit one must refer to the Islamic historical antecedents of the state, and their concepts of law and authority. I have already alluded to the difficulty the concept of nation-state encountered in the region because of the procrustean cultural bed created by the marriage of religion and politics, and where authority and law derive from other than a human source, so that abstract conceptions of a Law of Nature or Reason from which can flow such notions as individual human rights do not exist. Nor do those of corporate personalities, with some qualifications and rare exceptions. In short, the nation in the historical experience of the Arabs, and wider afield, the Muslims, at least till the nineteenth century, was not consciously territorial, but ideological.[4]

The fact remains that in recent history, all the above-mentioned states used nationalism in order to do two things. Firstly, they tried to create a consensus of sorts within their respective boundaries based on nationalism (in varying degrees). Secondly, they tried to create a consensus among a number of Arab states for the formation of a wider Arab nation-state (essence and practical expression of pan-Arabism).

One could argue in this connection that in the Arabian Peninsula and the Gulf at its eastern extremity, the oil-wealth that allows for industrialization is also supporting a process which will theoretically at least, transform traditional, tribal states into nation-states through a genuine allegiance to new institutional structures. Yet in view of lingering irredentist claims and counter-claims between these states, firm and final boundaries between them have yet to be agreed upon. Then the question of who is a citizen of these states remains to be properly defined.

Nevertheless (at least until a decade or two ago), the process everywhere in the Islamic world was one of the consolidation of nation-states. In several of them, religion had been in retreat; in one of them, Egypt, for a good 150 years from 1820 to 1970; and in Turkey from 1830 to 1955.

Arab nationalism served as the catalyst, if not standard-bearer in a process of regularizing the state and society in parts of the Islamic world. It was even tried as an ideology for development. In retrospect though, one must concede that it failed as a credible, creative political ideology in Islamic societies; that is why one cannot use it to explain political processes and political behaviour in those states. Furthermore, whatever nationalism may or may not have achieved, it is now being challenged by militant religious movements. As the supreme manifestation of political secularism, nationalism is at bay as a result of the forceful challenge that militant or radical Islam presents. In fact it is under attack from both sectarian and mainstream Islam.

The failure of radical, secular Arab nationalism in 1967 and the emergence of a wealthy constellation of oil-exporting Muslim states, suggested to many that Arab nationalism could be better served and promoted without its secular component. Rather they favoured the religious conception of the nation, the *umma*, as being more efficacious. Recent events, however, suggest that these too are inadequate, not up to the task, although Lebanon is not a good example, since it comprises a sizable population that does not belong to the *umma*, the nation of Islam. One observes, moreover, that both Arab and religious nationalism and political Islam have remained spectators in the Gulf War between two Islamic states. Recently, a presumably Arab country destroyed itself in a brutal civil war and Arab nationalism had precious little to say about it. Forty years ago, a militant and militarily powerful non-Arab state, *Israel*, proceeded with impunity to decimate and disperse an indigenous Arab community (Muslim in the main) and pacify its Arab neighbours by force, and neither secular Arab nationalism nor the more traditional variant of ideology (militant Islam) was able to stop.

Secularism, and the difficulties it has faced in the world of Islam, lies at the centre of the problem of Islam and the nation-state. In his recently published monograph on the debate regarding the application of the *sharia*, Husein Ahmad Amin introduces a detailed discussion of the issue into the debate.[5] He considers briefly a survey of the rise of secularism in Christian Europe, arguing that secularism represents an attempt to free human knowledge from the constraints of metaphysics and the unknown or occult, and that to that extent the famous tract *Fasl al-maqál fí má bayna'l-ḥikma wa'l-sharí'a min al-iṭṭiṣāl* by Averroes greatly influenced the thought of Thomas Aquinas, followed by Duns Scotus and William of Ockham, which helped separate and distinguish rational knowledge from faith or belief, and science from faith or revelation. Cartesian rationalism and the new age of seventeenth-century science marked the end of the Middle Ages and church monopoly over human endeavour. Machiavelli in the Renaissance established the right of the prince to govern independently of the Church. Luther and Calvin of the Protestant and Reformation movements, and the European Enlightenment that followed, gave a new important role to human science and the new middle classes against the Church, so that the nineteenth and twentieth centuries worked for the triumph of secularism and 'secular Christianity'.

Husein Amin contrasts this long-term development and struggle between modern or post-medieval European man with his new science and technology on the one hand, and the heavy restraining hand of a powerful Church defending a changing, dying order on the other, with the absence of such a conflict in Islam. After all, there was and is no Church in Islam, nor a clerical hierarchy provided for by the faith. Consequently, there could be no monopoly of knowledge by a non-existent group, class or institution. Nor was there a distinction made in the scripture (the Koran) between temporal and spiritual affairs. Islam has one *imam*, who is leader of both prayer and war. Nothing in the Koran is opposed to earthly or temporal good. And there is no religious authority set up in order to subjugate temporal institutions in Islam. Rather it is a simple faith: it has no need for a clergy specialized in interpreting a complex creed, or in interceding with God on behalf of the believers. And yet Islam acquired an elaborate, powerful class or caste of interpreters of the religious law, the *sharia*, as powerful in their desire to control the community of the faithful and as opposed to change brought about by human science as any Christian clergy in medieval Europe ever was. They developed a vast corpus of religious sciences, especially about the Sacred Law, and their special relation to rulers afforded them a privileged social and economic status and position, wielding great influence over the judicial, educational and social affairs of society.

As such it was in the interest of the religious establishment to promote and defend religious orthodoxy, educational formalism and rigid traditionalism on the pretext of protecting the Islamicity of the community. They put themselves forward as the interpreters and defenders of the faith, and the Islamic consciences of the *imams*. One of the most crucial factors in maintaining their position was their idealization of the past against the encroachment of modernity; their constant escape into the past; the veneration of the 'fathers'. A wider impact of this example offered by the bastion of tradition was the widespread romantic view held by Muslims in general of their past, past men and events. This is not a mere idle interpretation of how the men of religion sustained their key position as defenders of tradition, as good or bad as any other interpreter. On the contrary, it is crucial in understanding its use by Radical (militant) Islam today. It is through this romantic version of the past and the fathers that militant Islamic movements today try to appeal to and attract recruits, especially when the idealized past contrasts so favourably with the rotten and corrupt present condition of the *umma*, the Islamic nation. Husein Amin suspects that such an approach by militant organizations is not one that would be preferred by someone who means to seek and provide solutions for the problems of his society; in fact, it is the position of someone who wishes to stupefy a people that have failed to solve their problems in order to attract them to these militant organizations.

On a broader front, this process is assisted further by contemporary Islamic historians who also indulge in anachronistic interpretations of the past — Marxist or otherwise. That is, historians who distort the facts to fit their ideological preferences or predilections.

The question, indeed challenge, which Husein Amin poses to both the official religious establishment, the guardian of tradition, and the radical Islamic militant is: Why be like the fathers at all? And what is so great about the past? He is not suggesting that the past be execrated, only that it not be misrepresented and misinterpreted anachronistically or romantically.

The thrust of Husein Amin's argument which merits attention is that there is nothing in the Islamic faith, its religious doctrine, or scripturally prescribed organization that opposes and forbids secularism or a secularist approach to the affairs of state and society. Rather, historical experience, events, developments and deliberate choices by Muslims have given rise to a particular elite in the community which has set itself up as the guardian of religious tradition and the enemy of any innovation or change based on human knowledge or science. But this is not an integral part of the Muslim creed. Husein Amin is also implying that if this nexus were removed, the appeal of militant Islamic movements would diminish accordingly. Stretched to its logical conclusion, Husein's argument postulates that (1) there is no need for something Muslims call the Islamic state, and (2) there is no such institution anyway, primarily because Islam and Muslims do not need it in order to survive and live or conduct Muslim lives. For Husein Amin, there is no contradiction between Islam and the nation-state. The only other contemporary Egyptian Islamic writers who could be placed in Husein Amin's corner are the judge, Said Ashmawi,[6] and the other leading secularists already mentioned in passing.

If Husein Amin's position, acceptable or not, were applied, it would not eliminate the state's or the ruler's periodic leaning on the Islamic crutch. They will still involve the religion for their own political purposes, and solicit the support of the religious establishment. This for domestic purposes. On the international level, they may even find greater and more frequent excuse (or cause) to appeal to the Islamic dimension.

The difficulty may not be one of public secularism at the level of the state. It may well be one of individual secular attitudes at the level of the individual Muslim. The emphasis in Islam has been mostly on certain notions of justice and morality, of Muslim conduct in public, and less on individual or personal morality. This is a matter for Muslim philosophers and deontologists to sort out for themselves.

For 1,400 years now the separation between the religious ideal and the historical reality of the Islamic nation, so avidly pursued and maintained by the doctors of law and the religious teachers, especially since the Abbasid period, has prevailed. The guardians of religious tradition remained victorious over the historians, so much so that the corruption of Muslim historiography was represented by the persistently romantic view of Islamic history held by most Muslims. The Ottoman hegemony over the Islamic realm led to the death of thought, and intellectual inertia and stagnation. Muslims were overwhelmed by highly organized formal religious teaching, controlled by a privileged class of religious teachers who also became the recognized censors of all Islamic thought and action, at a time when the Christian Church in Europe was fast losing this role and function. Even today it is still difficult and hazardous for non-religious scholars to study or inquire into religious matters.[7]

The weakest part of Husein Amin's argument in this discussion of secularism is perhaps the one that tries to ascribe the historical, romantic streak to the nature of the Arab mind or to the Arab's intellectual formation: that it is exaggerative, sharply dichotomous between black and white and allowing for no grey area. Is that the effect of the desert, Husein Amin wonders, and its impact on the Arab's modes of thought where he moves from repose, calm, surrender and dependence (presumably on God, fate, whatever) *suddenly* to an emotional destructive explosion?

He gives the same explanation for the Arab's lack of precision (imprecise thought) and concludes that exaggeration 'is a cultural feature or manifestation of certain social and economic conditions'. Hence the escape to idealized images of his past, a kind of wishful thinking to assuage the miserable reality of the present. The Arab or Muslim, in short, is obsessed by his own history. But so are many other non-Muslim peoples and societies.

Despite the formal rejection of secularism by radical Islam and the discrediting of nationalism as an ideology in recent years, the restored ideological primacy of Islam has not reduced either the intensity or level of conflict in the *umma*, the nation of Islam. In some respects it has, on the contrary, intensified intra-*umma* conflict. Nor has it provided greater cohesion and cooperation among Muslims.

For a decade at least (1956–66) intra-*umma* conflict over secular state interests was dominated in the Arab part of the *umma* by the hostility and rivalry between Egypt and Saudi Arabia. Presented to the Arab public as a contest between two essentially and ostensibly secular political movements, revolution versus reaction, the contest was in fact over the control of an important section of the *umma*, or nation of Islam. A corollary and parallel conflict was the one between Cairo and Amman, Nasser of Egypt and King Hussein of Jordan and the pre-1958 monarchy in Iraq, popularly presented in the search for the allegiance of an ill-defined Arab public as one between two political orders, monarchy and republic. These conflicts spilled over into neighbouring states; in the case of Egypt versus Saudi Arabia, into the Yemen, and in that of Cairo versus Amman and Baghdad, into Syria, Lebanon and Iraq. Yet in both cases, these conflicts were a continuation of earlier rivalries and contests between two Muslim states going back in history at least to the early 1920s, regardless of their common membership in the *umma*, the nation of Islam. Secular state interest, even disparate experience as nation-states, aspirations to leadership and ascendancy in the Muslim Arab world, took precedence over their common religious identity. In short, religion as a political ideology was inadequate, and could be easily overlooked, violated, or ignored, even when the rivalry and hostility were clothed or articulated in religious terms.

Are we witnessing contests between rival ideologies extrapolated from the religion of Islam? Or are we seeing the conflict between rival national-state interests, as these are perceived and formulated by national-state rulers, formulated or expressed in religious terms and put forward as Islamic political ideologies? If this is the case, the position insisted upon by radical Muslim ideologues that Islam presents the best political order for the Muslim whoever he is and wherever he may be, collapses. At best it can be salvaged by reformulation: as a basis for public morality and public order, Islam is even more problematic than its secular ideological counterparts. As a basis for private morality and a public ethic it has yet to be given a chance. And so the historical and perennial ambivalence and confusion continue.

Considering more recent events of the last few years one can even speak about a recurrence or reappearance of sectarian conflict in the *umma*, the nation of Islam. However one may wish to avoid it, one cannot honestly ignore an underlying Sunni (PLO) versus Shii (Amal and others) conflict in Lebanon, especially Sidon in the south and Tripoli in the north, as well as an heretical Alawite versus strictly orthodox or Sunni conflict within Syria under the regime headed by President Hafiz al-Asad.

There may be no historian, religious polemicist like Baghdadi or Shahrastani of the twentieth century to produce the usual polemical tracts on this intra-*umma* sectarian conflict as yet, but the Iran-Iraq war, originally over a territorial dispute in the Gulf, is the major sectarian conflict in Islam in over half a millennium.[8]

Where Islam was proclaimed as the preferred basis and ideology of the political order, the state, as in the recent case of Iran, does not appear to have reduced, let alone eliminated, either domestic or external conflict. Nor has it engendered the much vaunted economic and social benefits it promised.

Of course conflict between Muslim states is not a recent development. It dates from the earliest period of Islamic history. State interest became a primary consideration of policy from the time the second Caliph, Omar b. al-Khattab (634–44) created the earliest administrative-political institutions of the Islamic state; that is, as a result of his creative structural political reform. At that early stage in the evolution of the political dominion of Islam by conquest, such 'state interest' frequently coincided — was even synonymous — with the interest of the nation of Islam, that is, the *umma*. Therefore, it could easily be accommodated, expressed by Islam as political ideology, Islam or religion as the exclusive basis of political order.

It is interesting that Abu al-Hasan al-Nadvi, one of the authors who have greatly influenced the leading ideologues of radical Islam, such as Sayyid Qutb, explains the decline of Islam and the Muslims mainly in terms of loss of earthly power.[9] Himself an *ʿalim* in Lucknow, India, and Azhar-trained, Nadvi argues in his book that Islam is an uplifting, superior creed. Therefore it cannot be subordinated to other creeds; it must, alone, prevail and be on top. Nor can it cooperate with others in order to reform society or the world. The Muslims have been delegated by God to lead the world and humanity; they cannot be led by others. Note the insistence by Nadvi on the superiority and exclusiveness of Islam *vis-à-vis* all other faiths and systems. His book represents the clearest statement about the difference between the Islamic and non-Islamic views of the world, and the reasons why Islam must once again become the exclusively dominant perception, creed and world view. To this extent Nadvi's statement is also a firm *rejection* of the non-Islamic perception.

In his book *al-Islam, wa al-uruba, wa al-ilmaniyya* (Islam, Arabism and Secularism), Dr Muhammad ʿImara attacked those who argue in favour of the contradiction between Islam and Arabism (Arab nationalism).[10] Such an argument, he claims, has arisen only in the period of decline, '. . . when Mamlukes attained power in the Arab countries. As they were Muslims and not Arabs, they made the religious bond a substitute — in fact, a negation — of the Arab bond'. Ottomans after them followed the same route. When the colonialists marched on the Arab lands and the world of Islam, they played the same game, exploiting the presumed contradiction between the religious and the national bond in order to strike at Arabism and Islam and so conquer and occupy both the Arab countries and the Muslims. At one time these Europeans supported Muhammad Ali's 'Arab project', and when he appeared close to succeeding in its implementation, they opposed him in conjunction with Ottoman Islam. Subsequently (e.g. in the Great War), they supported Arabism in the East against the Islam of the Ottomans. At the same time they divided (shared among themselves) the Arab nation that had emerged from the Great War, having managed to abolish the Islamic Caliphate (in Istanbul) and the project of the Arab nation-state. Then, in confronting Islamic thought, they sowed the seeds of secularism and Westernization among the Arabs. More recently, in combating the radical Nasserite Arab nationalist expansionist movement, they sought to set up regional alliances under the banner of Islam.

The thrust of Dr ʿImara's argument is that non-Arab Muslims who controlled power for several centuries not only caused the decline of the Arabs, but also created the dichotomy between Islam and Arabism. The dichotomy surely dates from an earlier stage in the history of Islam. It was the Prophet Muhammad who offered Islam as the new bond holding the community of the believers together and replacing the older bond of blood characteristic of Arab tribalism which prevailed before Islam. Furthermore, the strict orthodox Muslims, including the interpreters and upholders of the Sacred Law (the *sharia*), as well as the more militant exponents of radical Islam who now clamour for the return of religion to the centre of political life, insist on the incompatibility between Islam and the secular idea of Arab nationalism; for them, Islam is still the exclusive basis of national identity, the *umma*, or community of the faithful, the only nation to which a Muslim belongs. At the same time, such a Muslim does not deny the idea of patriotism, one's loyalty to one's own country: he does not think it undermines or contradicts loyalty to Islam. The fact remains that there has been, so far, no final resolution between all these several levels of loyalty. The matter remains part of the unresolved wider issue of Islam and politics, Islam and the state.

5

The Obstacles to Plural Politics and a Pluralist Polity in Islam: Non-Muslims in a Muslim Society

Western secularists agree that one of the attractive — and desirable — features of the secular nation-state is that of political pluralism. The classically formulated and generally accepted position of non-Muslims in Muslim society, however, seems to preclude, at least theoretically, political pluralism in the nation-state.

A recent book on non-Muslims in Muslim society is by Dr Yusuf al-Qardawi.[2] A prolific writer on Islamic themes and closely associated with the Society of Muslim Brothers, Dr Qardawi is an *'alim* and a *faqih*; that is, someone well versed in the study of Islamic Law, theology and jurisprudence.[3] What is interesting is that in the same year a book by Gamal Badawi appeared on the communal disturbances in Egypt.[4] Only a year before that, the Copt, Dr William Suleiman, published his *Debate between Religions*.[5] Tariq al-Bishri's series of articles in *al-Tali'a*, 'Misr bayna Ahmad wa'l-Masih', was published in the 1970s, culminating in his book, *al-Muslimun wa'l-aqbat fi itar al-jama'a al-wataniyya*.[6] The public debate between Tawfiq al-Hakim and Louis Awad, representing secular Egyptian nationalism on one side and their pro-Arab nationalism detractors and interlocutors on the other, was published in Cairo in 1981 under the title *al-In'izaliyyun fi Misr* (The Isolationists in Egypt). The writings of a leading Azharite and Muslim Brother sympathizer, Dr Muhammad al-Bahiy, on Islamic thought and contemporary society of the mid-1960s, were reprinted in new editions.[7] A thesis for Cairo University by Muhammad Shawqi Zaki published in 1980 was given wide publicity.[8] In the same year, the Coptic writer, Milad Hanna's *Copts yes, but none the less Egyptians*, was given equally wide publicity.[9] Similarly, the works of Dr Abdel Hamid Metwalli on the crisis of Islamic political thought throughout the 1970s were widely read.[10] And this is only a very small sample of the proliferation of the more sophisticated and detailed works on Islam and society. But there is also the unending stream of popular booklets and tracts on Islam which litter sidewalk newsstands and bookstalls in the major cities and towns of Egypt.

These writings of the 1970s and early 1980s are an attempt to build and gloss on the earlier writings of the 'masters', such as Hasan al-Banna, Sayyid Qutb, Muhammad al-Ghazali, Abdel Qadir Auda and other leading personages of the Society of Muslim Brothers. In arguing the case and calling for the construction of an Islamic society and political order, guided by the word of God and governed by His revealed law, all of these writers, without exception, oppose secular political orders (*'ilmaniyya*) as belonging to the 'age of ignorance' (*jahiliyya*) and as having an infidel provenance from the West and East alike. They all argue that these are unacceptable, for a Muslim can lead a believer's life only in an Islamic state and society; that he must not obey any other man-made law, or those who legislate and enforce it.[11] The separation between the true believer and such 'materialist' transient orders is complete and unbridgeable. At the same time, all these writers feel constrained to touch upon the subject of non-Muslims, the so-called *ahl al-dhimma*, in an Islamic political order. They invariably defend the doctrinal, i.e. Koranic, revelations about this matter, ignore the record of historical experience, and assert that the true condition and correct position of non-Muslims in Muslim society are reflected in these revealed instructions and the administrative record of the first four Orthodox Caliphs. This, they contend further, is ample evidence and guarantee for the possibility of pluralism in an Islamic order. It is, therefore, useful and instructive to survey briefly the stated position regarding this matter as formulated, argued and presented by some of these writers before offering any comment on some of the basic principles that may be derived from such an exposition.

Although Gibb and Bowen concluded the two parts of their study *Islamic Society and the West*[12] with a long chapter on *dhimmis* — that is, the recognized, tolerated religious and ethnic minorities in the Ottoman empire — they only touch upon the doctrinal position. Otherwise, their work dealt specifically with the corporate nature of the *millet* in the Ottoman state, and the history of the relations between these communities, or minorities, and the Ottoman government. The only monographic study in English of the relation between non-Muslim subjects and their Muslim rulers is that by Professor A.S. Tritton, published nearly 55 years ago.[13] After a careful consideration of original sources, beginning with the Caliph Omar's 'covenant', Tritton concluded,

> This study of the relations between the government and its subjects who did not profess Islam can only produce confusion in the mind. At one moment the *dhimmi* appears as a persecuted worm who is entirely negligible, and the next complaint is made of his pernicious influence on the Muslims round him . . . There is no constitutional growth; events move in irregular curves, not in a straight line (p. 229) . . . The rule of Islam was often burdensome, the revolts in Egypt prove it (p. 230) . . . Restrictions were placed on their dress, and the attempt to oust them from official posts began (pp. 230–1).

Recognizing that individual Christians and Jews were often close to the ruler and sometimes held the highest posts, Tritton goes on to say, 'Though *dhimmis* might enjoy great prosperity, yet always they lived on sufferance, exposed to the caprices of the rulers and the passions of the mob' (232). Remarking on the eventual spiritual isolation of Islam, he notes, 'The world was divided into two classes, Muslims and others, and only Islam counted' (232).

In 1947, Albert Hourani published his *Minorities in the Arab World* under the auspices of the Royal Institute of International Affairs.[14] It dealt mainly with Egypt and the Fertile Crescent. The latter comprised relatively recent states under British and French mandate. But these states were also encumbered by a high proportion of minorities, reflecting ethnic and sectarian diversity. After considering the status and condition of these minorities in each country, guarantees for their protection and their freedom of religious practice, the impact of nationalism in both its secular Arab and Islamic varieties, as well as the historical tradition of fear, suspicion and resentment between the various communities, Hourani concluded that the majority and the minorities did not fully constitute a national community in any of these countries. In enumerating problems of intermarriage, conversion, and civil and political equality, he wondered if secular nationalism was sufficient basis for a national community and stable government. Moreover, neither assimilation nor autonomy seemed to Hourani at the time to constitute permanent solutions to the problem. In examining the historical, religious and demographic reasons for so massive a presence of minorities, he observed that non-Muslims (Christians and Jews) did not form part of the community of the state, i.e. the body politic. He also noted that these were closed communities, 'all marginal, shut out from power and historic decision'.[15]

Gibb and Bowen later in 1950 defined a *dhimmi* as a non-Muslim subject of a Muslim ruler. Relations with the ruler are regulated by contract once the non-Muslim community is incorporated in the Domain of Islam. Under special conditions the contract provides for the toleration of the infidel *dhimmi* and allows him to practise his religion. They emphasize, therefore, the division between believers and infidels both in Islamic society and in the world. But even under this contract, what is offered the non-Muslim is in return for the payment of a special poll tax (*jizya*: abolished in the Ottoman state in 1855 and in Egypt in 1856) and the agreement to suffer certain restrictions. The identification *dhimmi* refers to the member of a caste inferior to his Muslim fellow subjects. He must suffer legal disadvantages, at times be subject to certain laws regarding distinctive clothing, and refrain from the building of new churches or places of worship unless he complies with certain specific regulations.[16] In such a political order, *dhimmis* are not dealt with by the government as individual citizens or subjects of the state, but as members of a distinct and separate community. The status, the rights and duties of the *dhimmi* therefore derive exclusively from his membership of a protected community. Needless to say, the *millet* idea was not an original invention of the Muslims or the Ottomans. Romans and Byzantines practised such discrimination between the *homoioi* and the others, especially by the Byzantines as regards the Jews.

After a lengthy discussion of the history of these minorities and how they fared in their relations with the state, Gibb and Bowen conclude that the essence of *dhimmi* status is one of inferiority. They further enumerate certain consequences of the classification in Islam of *dhimmis* by religion. One of these militated against the solidarity of the Ottoman society; another discouraged primary loyalty to the Sultan since such political loyalty was subordinated to the primordial attachment to the religious or ethnic community. Although in the rural areas the distinction between *dhimmi* and Muslim tended to fade away, in the urban centres the distinction and separation were pronounced. Consequently, integration was difficult and not encouraged either by the Muslim ruler or the leaders of the various non-Muslim communities for economic and other reasons. Finally, while the *sharia* enjoins the toleration of scriptural infidels, it insists on their inferiority.[17]

What one can infer from these studies is firstly, that originally the relationship between non-Muslim subjects and Muslim rulers was contractual. Secondly, that there was no systematic legal development either to regulate this relationship or to integrate the non-Muslims into the Islamic polity. The nearest thing to a regularized system was the Ottoman *millet*, which, if anything, consecrated and institutionalized the separateness of the *dhimmi* from the larger society and political order. Lastly, much of the status and condition of this relationship depended in the final analysis on the individual ruler.

Until the mid-1960s, the question of non-Muslims in Muslim society did not attract the attention, or engage the energies, of Arab Muslim writers, apart from the known tracts of the leaders of the Ikhwan. (I am using the term Ikhwan interchangeably with Muslim Brethren.) This may have been due in part to the Arab nationalist and generally radical euphoria of the fifties and early sixties under the leadership of Nasser in Egypt and the Baath in the Fertile Crescent. As I have already indicated, more recent literature is keen on the subject, suggesting that, now that secular political ideas in the Middle East have been devalued and are in retreat and their exponents on the defensive — some of these writers, in fact, anticipate a rout of secularism — the only possible alternative is the restoration of an Islamic political order throughout the region.

My purpose in this preliminary discussion is not to comment on specific instances of the history of minorities in Islamic countries. Nor is it to define and analyze the phenomenon of ethnic diversity in this part of the world. Rather it is to highlight the doctrinal basis — and confusion — of religious pluralism and its political negation, i.e. the failure to accommodate it politically. In doing so, I shall also refer — only in passing — to the difference between an asserted support and protection of pluralism on the basis of the scriptures on the one hand, and its indifferent fate in actual practice, or at least historical experience, on the other. In short, I propose to assist in defining the religious-social-political environment and (shaky?) foundation upon which such religio-political pluralism exists, and to what extent it is only a putative political pluralism.

By ethnicity I suppose we mean a diversity of ethnic groups or 'nations' within the territorial boundaries of a state. Of course, this may not preclude the existence of the same ethnic group across state boundaries, as is the case of, say, the Kurds. I do not propose to deal with this phenomenon in the Middle East. Pluralism, on the other hand, I take to mean religious and cultural diversity within and across state boundaries. In Western political usage, however, it refers to the private and public acceptance of opposing political views, promoted by freely organized voluntary associations, interest groups and political parties, and the toleration of alternative governments or regimes. There are a few regimes today (mostly in the West) which subscribe to values that uphold a plural political system. There are many others, especially in the Middle East, which do not subscribe to or at least are unable to construct plural political systems even though the society in them is characterized by ethnic diversity and religious pluralism. They simply have been unable politically to accommodate this diversity.[18]

One of them, Lebanon, which constructed its political system on a confessional basis, has recently disintegrated. That particular crisis has been

> . . . a manifestation of a wider, more general, political problem in the Middle East, where religion is a potent ideological force which challenges territorial rule. The religion-based identity of Middle Easterners has resisted the secular integration of nationalism, and politics itself has been understood and regarded as a variant of religion.[19]

In a succinct and concise essay, 'Religion and Secular Nationalism in the Arab World',[20] Professor Elie Kedourie underlined the clash between nationalism in which the 'primordial value is the nation, not, say, class or religion', and other ideological conceptions of the nation. When Islam became the expression of Arab national genius and was thus inexorably linked to Arabism, the secular trend of the nineteenth and early twentieth centuries was abandoned in favour of an older dichotomy, the one between the solidarity of a superior Islamic nation and all other political systems. This suggests that the more rigid the ideological definition of a nation or political order, the more difficult its accommodation of ethnic and religious diversity within its territorial boundaries become. As for political pluralism, it is rejected outright by such a total ideological order since the political system separates the non-Muslim from the body politic by tolerating him, if he is a *dhimmi*, as a member of a separate community.[21]

By looking into the matters of ethnicity and pluralism I hope to delineate or define Islam's and the Muslims' perceptions of them, and to consider in what kind of political order they can be accommodated and, more specifically, whether the Muslim doctrinal provisions and historical perceptions render such accommodation easy, difficult or impossible. Thus, if Islam and those who claim to represent it and wish to implement its law and rule over man, society and the polity, reject all other human forms of law and rule and insist on the necessity of a total, i.e. all-embracing, ideological purity and uniformity, then clearly there is an unbridgeable gap between them and all other social and political arrangements. In practice, this has taken the form of a conflict between the adapters of secular temporal political arrangements and the champions of the rule of God on earth; between, on the one hand, those who contend that a Muslim can be a believer, a member of the *umma* and a carrier of Islamic culture and still organize his earthly public life on the basis of man-made law; and, on the other, those who insist that one is not a Muslim by any definition unless he establishes the law of God as the only regulator of his earthly life. The former, theoretically at least, accepts the integration of a national community and body politic that includes non-Muslims as full members. Public affairs are regulated by a uniform law of the land; authority and power are territory-based. The latter rejects all of this outright, and refers to divine dispensation regarding non-Muslims in the *umma*, since the latter recognizes no territorial boundaries, only the bond of faith. Any society that is governed by and governs according to anything other than God's law is an infidel one. No person can really lead the life of a true Muslim except in such an Islamic state.[22]

This in brief is the main thrust and argument of all the writings by the proponents of the Islamic state and rule until today. And it is within this context that they deal with — or ignore — the question of non-Muslims. Yet, interestingly enough, their argument begins with the issue of power on the basis of the Suras:[23]

> They say: Surely, if we return to al-Madinah the mightier will soon drive out the weaker; when might belongeth to Allah and to His Messenger and the believers; but the hypocrites know not (Sura lxiv, *al-Munafiqun*: 8)
> . . . and Allah will not give the disbelievers any way of success against the believers (Sura iv, *Women*: 141)
> And fight them until persecution is no more, and religion is all for Allah . . . (Sura viii, *Anfal*: 39)

In fact, Hasan al-Banna proclaimed: 'We demand power for all of us',[24] until the Muslims raise the 'banner of the Koran everywhere'.[25] People are clearly divided under this power between believers and unbelievers. In the end though, 'God must inherit the earth', so that, while protecting non-Muslims, the believer must not cease to call upon them to embrace the true faith and submit to God's perfect law.[26] Since Islam is there and available no other order on earth will do. Power, after all, is the symbol of Islam, and earthly government one of its pillars. The first requirement in the establishment of such an order, therefore, is the transformation of society from a powerless Islamic one to one in which power is monopolized by the Muslims in it.[27]

Qardawi states baldly that the legal position of non-Muslims in Muslim society is that they have the same rights and duties as the Muslims except in certain clearly defined exceptional cases. Their special position, as *dhimmis*, is based on revelation providing a covenant from God, the Prophet and the community (*umma*) which guarantees them protection and security. They are granted citizenship on certain conditions: payment of the *jizya* and observance of the *sharia* in all matters other than religion. Otherwise, they are members of the Domain of Islam (*dar al-islam*). While they have the right to protection against external enemies and internal oppression, social security, freedom of worship, freedom of work and profit (but not from *riba*, usury and interest), the right to hold official state posts other than religious ones (these are enumerated as the *imama*, head of state, leadership of the armed forces, judicial posts entailing adjudication between Muslims, and the administration of *waqfs*), they must respect Islam and the religious feelings of Muslims by not displaying prominently their own religious symbols and not erect churches or synagogues in places where they had none before.[28] The difficulty of course arises over the guarantees for these rights of non-Muslims. The *sharia* enjoins them upon the believers, and the *imam* and the community must observe the law. Yet in the end the only guarantee is that of the Muslim's conscience.

A fair point made by Qardawi and many others is that as citizens of an Islamic state, non-Muslims must observe all the laws that do not affect their religious belief and freedom of worship: civil, criminal and commercial. But they cannot preach beliefs that are contrary to Islam, the religion of the state; that is, they cannot hold, entertain or publish opposing or differing views and beliefs. This position, incidentally, is common to all other writers on the subject. They all extol the unique tolerance of non-Muslims by Islam, in doctrine and practice, in sharp contrast to the persecution of religious minorities, especially the Jews, in Christian Europe. They all invariably assert this despite, as they admit, the historical record. This is due partly to their perception of the Islamic state as being similar to that in existence at the time of the Prophet and the four Orthodox Caliphs. But Qardawi complains,

> It is not part of forgiveness to ask of the Muslim to forego and freeze his religious rules and the law of God . . . the destruction of his religious guide to life for the sake of non-Muslim minorities so as not to cause them anxiety or hurt their feelings.[29]

If the rules of his faith bring the Muslim closer to his God, non-Muslims must accept them as the law of the land, and obey the state order that is accepted by the majority.[30] It is not toleration to substitute nationalism for these rules since nationalism is contrary to Islam — and Christianity.[31] Islamic society is based on a belief and an ideology from which flow the ethic and rules of conduct.[32] God prohibits the Muslim from governing by or obeying any law except His own. No other social and political 'bond' (for example, nationalism) is permissible, or can replace that of religion. The Muslim cannot allow or live under an administration or political order controlled by non-Muslims.[33]

It is on the basis of the above notions that most of these writers try to explain away, albeit unconvincingly, the occasional special laws applied to *dhimmis* for purposes of social distinction, and the periodic hostility of Muslims to *dhimmis* as well as the uprisings against them. They justify their hostility to a secular order by the belief that secularism has been 'the octopus which destroyed Islamic society and its values'.[34] At the same time, they link their insistence upon an Islamic order with independence from an infidel world, their liberation from its deleterious ideas, and their right based on impressive potential power. Thus there are some 37 to 40 independent Islamic countries, occupying very strategic locations in the world — the Suez Canal, the Dardanelles, the Red Sea and the Gulf. They control over 60 per cent of proven oil reserves, 70 per cent of rubber, and 50 per cent of jute. Sixty per cent of Mediterraneans are Muslim. One fifth of the world's population is Muslim. Of about 41 African states, 23 are Muslim with nearly 60 per cent of the continent's population. In other words, it is the feeling of growing and potential power which encourages the demand for an Islamic order.

Abdel Hamid Metwalli, a prolific contemporary writer, and one who supports the idea of an Islamic order, recognizes nevertheless the crisis in Islamic political thought arising from the abject emulation by Muslims of the West in the conduct of their public affairs and the tyranny of despotic rule in Islamic countries.[35] But despite his attempt at a liberal interpretation of doctrine and law, he rejects the notions of popular sovereignty and elections as non-Islamic concepts. Political choice in this order will be denied to non-Muslims since they will remain outside the body politic.

The Islamic order, with its doctrinal provisions for non-Muslims, is also viewed by many of these writers as necessary in order to combat alien, infidel ideologies. It is an aspect of the ideological and political separation between what is Muslim and what is non-Muslim. God made the Muslims, not anyone else, as His vicegerents on earth in order that they rule and govern. After all, Allah's religion is Islam,[36] and nothing else will do.[37] Rule belongs to God; all other rule is infidel and must be rejected. The constitution of the *sharia* is universal, good for the whole world. Islamic rule is legitimate, all other rule is tyranny and despotism. Unbelief (*kufr*) is synonymous with tyranny (*zulm*).[38] It is in the nature of Islam to be superior and dominate all else.[39] Islamic precepts are not implemented by individuals, but by states and governments.[40]

Although he utters the usual pious formulae about the equality between Muslims and *dhimmis*, Abdel Qadir Auda, a leading member of the Muslim Brotherhood's Supreme Council until his execution in 1954, for instance, suggests there is no possibility of a civil society in Islam, only a religious-ideological one. And while the *sharia* for him, and others like him, has universal applicability, its actual implementation is possible only where Muslims hold power; that is, in the Domain of Islam (*dar al-islam*). Circumstances, in the meantime, have rendered it regional rather than universal. The citizens of the *dar al-islam* are of two categories: those who embrace Islam the faith, and those who abide by its rules without however embracing the faith; that is, the *dhimmis*.

It cannot be emphasized enough that the Islamic order is being put forward as the imperative total alternative to a plural system. It is perhaps for this reason that non-Muslim minorities remain anxious and apprehensive. Given also the fact that temporal regimes have failed to construct political orders wholly detached from religion (that is, provide a distinct alternative to Islam as *din wa dawla*), pluralism has suffered even more, and the feeling of political separation on the part of minorities has persisted. This trend is most pronounced in the writings of the late Sayyid Qutb of the Ikhwan throughout the 1950s and 1960s until his execution. For him, Islam is the only liberating force remaining in a perverted, corrupt world, and the political future belongs to it. He emphasizes the collective total society offered by Islam in contrast to the extreme individualism of Christianity and the exclusiveness of Judaism.[41] He even claims credit for Islam for inspiring the European movements of Humanism and the Renaissance. He is, alas, unaware of the Graeco-Roman roots of these movements. The failure of the actual historical experience and practice of Islam to attain the ideal Islamic order is, for Qutb, merely a transient abberation and deviation. While it is true, as Qutb contends, that Christianity is not a social theory and cannot be the basis of a social and political system — whereas Islam is and can — he ignores the more permanent ethical and metaphysical principles which influenced, or at least informed, the evolving order in

Europe. He also denies man any choice in devising a temporal order since the Islamic social system is original, created by revelation as a 'Godly order'. The historical forms which Islamic society has taken so far do not, according to Qutb, define, limit or exhaust all other possible forms of this society for every generation. It is a unique system because it was not founded by man, but by God's revealed law (*nizam kulli da'im*).[42]

Qutb makes the usual statements about non-Muslims, but he admits to religious fanaticism (*ta'aṣṣub*).[43] He goes further than other writers when he suggests that non-Muslims in Muslim society can submit to the general ethic (*manhaj*) based on the worship of God alone even though they are not Muslim.[44] At the same time, he is more Manichean in his sharp distinction between good (Islam) and evil (all else), and the two cannot co-exist. There is only one world, that of Islam, and no nation or country for a Muslim except one in which God's *sharia* reigns supreme.[45] The World of Islam is where everyone, including *dhimmis*, accepts the *sharia* as the regulator of private and public life. All lands where Islam is not in control of public order constitute the World of War, which is to be opposed and fought against by Muslims.[46] Qutb's dialectic, or dynamic, of constant struggle between the Muslim and non-Muslim is interesting because the latter also includes Muslims who refuse to set up a truly Islamic order on earth. There can be no compromise. Truth is absolute and indivisible.[47] The duty and role of Islam and the Muslim is to divest the world of *jahiliyya*-type leadership. There is one choice only — between unbelief (*kufr*) and belief (*iman*), tyranny and faith.[48]

Needless to say, Qutb's notorious tract, *Ma'alim fi al-tariq*, was a stirring call to action. Boldly explicit in its demand for power to be placed in the hands of a leader who is committed to the establishment of the Islamic order and state, as well as in his attack on the then regime in Egypt, it is no wonder he was arrested and executed. He was openly proclaiming his — and that of all true Muslims — disobedience of constituted authority and defying the power of the state.[49]

It is a fact that, despite all the difficulties, non-Muslims have survived in Muslim societies, states and empires for the last 1,400 years. One must note, however, that they did so mainly, and for most of that period, as separate, corporate communities in a special relationship with their Muslim rulers. Many of them

— on the unofficial, private level — have co-existed as infidel minorities relatively peacefully with the Muslim majority. A very small elite among them even reached high positions of state in the courts of Muslim rulers. But one must also note that, to some extent, from the sixteenth century to the Second World War, many of these communities enjoyed the protection of their more powerful co-religionists from Europe under special arrangements. In the inter-war period, and more recently at the height of nationalist fervour, several of them suffered the disabilities of ethnic and/or religious minorities, in Turkey, Iraq and elsewhere. The trend, though, was for newly established national governments to adopt secular forms, and at least affect the integration of all their inhabitant-subjects as citizens of a territorial nation-state. The attempt was confused, indeterminate and weakened by society's deep attachment to tradition. Lingering European power or influence acted for a while as some kind of guarantee against blatantly violent conflict between the majority and the minorities.

Egyptians, for example, proudly refer to their own efforts in the construction of a clearly secular national community, allowing for both ethnicity and pluralism, especially under the leadership of the Wafd. Yet even this singular and brief attempt was flawed because it was marred by tergiversation between the power and popularity returns of a less secular stand and the dangerous shoals of an uncharted secular sea. On the contrary, these clearly weak and hesitating champions of a secular public order, marked by a measure of political pluralism, were soon defeated by the return of traditional despotism, alongside a growing movement for an Islamic order. In fact, many of them had already succumbed to such an ethic. Secularism of the sword, however, remained; indeed it prospered. Secularism associated with the rule of a law not of divine provenance atrophied and collapsed. Greater deference to the Islamic ethos was demanded and given.[50]

It is in these conditions of failure, confusion and, in some respects, despair, that the sharpened — and violent — clash between the champions of a uniform, total Islamic order and the secular state (now no longer controlled by those initially willing to permit at least formal pluralism, but by powerful military and other autocrats) has been revived. Thus the failure of the nation-state in Lebanon is a matter of record. The persecution of religious minorities and opposition political groups by a proclaimed Islamic order in Iran is also a matter of record. The fear and insecurity of the Coptic minority in Egypt in the last 30 years led to an open confrontation between its leadership and the state in 1972, requiring the promulgation of the Law for the Protection of National Unity in August 1972.[51] Some Coptic writers frantically argued for a secular order in which a plural society could flourish and in which the essence of citizenship was allegiance to the nation, not religion. They called for an allegiance based on territory, language, a common life and shared historical experience.[52]

All of this suggests that Islamic protestations to the contrary notwithstanding, minorities remain anxious and apprehensive; sectarian conflict persists. If an Islamic order is, by definition as per the assertions of its proponents, a total system, it cannot entertain political pluralism, only political separation. No wonder then that non-Muslims were attracted in the past to secular solutions for the national community. Today, however, as a result of Islamic militancy and the demise of orders which at least theoretically allow pluralism, they are willing to consider for themselves a guaranteed separate status.

Muslim writers point to the awful persecution of minorities, especially the Jews, in Europe. Yet in the liberal democracies, the decision was made over 200 years ago to emancipate such minorities and treat them as full members of the body politic under a secular law of the land. Their rights and duties no longer derive from their separate status. Such a step is not one the proponents of the Islamic state propose to take. On the contrary, they simply wish to revert to the doctrinal provisions of the faith in so far as non-Muslims are concerned. In fact, according to the leading ones among them, only the law of God can prevail; all other sources of authority in society must be rejected. They insist on a 'Godly community' and a 'righteous political leadership' as the minimum requirement for a true Muslim religious and political life. Uniformity of conduct under the *sharia* must prevail over any, say, national integration, based on the political accommodation of ethnicity and pluralism. There must be one cultural tradition, the Islamic one, to guide and inspire the citizens of the Islamic state.[53] Nationalism is out.

There are also those who argue that the imposition of a righteous view of the public order insisted upon by some Muslims is simply a stage in the historical evolution of the societies. It is akin, or parallel to, say, that stage of the Cromwellian and Puritanical episode in seventeeth-century England; and that it is not a view, or position, that is peculiar, or endemic, to Islam. The analogy, in my view, is false. The Cromwellian revolution ended with the legislative ascendancy of parliament, the restoration of the monarchy and the supremacy of the civil law; it was soon followed by religious toleration, and later by gradual political emancipation; in short, by pluralism. Human values once more became the measure of a public order. Possibly the fact that Christianity does not provide in its doctrine any legal or juridical schemes for the regulation of the temporal relations between men, or the conduct of their earthly affairs, was an advantage. What is interesting is that Muslim writers recognize this and argue from it that, except in matters of faith and religious practice, non-Muslims in an Islamic order must come under the jurisdiction of the *sharia*.[54] This is a theoretically plausible proposition and one that, in the future, non-Muslims may have to consider as a serious possibility. On the other hand, when the same writers insist there are no human, only divine, values,[55] the possibility of pluralism becomes remote, because these values are eternal, immutable and final.

Surely, the essence of secularism, apart from the separation between religion and state, is the acceptance of the proposition that there is no finality to forms, no exclusive possession of absolute and indivisible truth. A corollary of this is the recognition of alternative notions about man and the world and, more significantly, the toleration of these alternative views. This implies scepticism, not certitude towards absolutist assertions, and experimentation with alternative forms. If this is a fair distinction between secularism and a total, ideological-divine order, then the essence of the problem of ethnicity and pluralism remains its political accommodation — or non-accommodation — in the state, and today in the territorially defined nation-state.

The problems of ethnicity and pluralism are not of course confined to the Middle East, or to Muslim societies. The peculiarity of their conflict-generating history may derive only in part from Islamic exclusiveness: the insistence upon the implementation of God's law on earth, and the sharp distinction between what is Muslim and what is not. It is nevertheless endemic to the conjoining of a universal religious message, or truth, and a particular community and social order on earth. In short, it arises from the sanctification of temporal power. To this extent, contrary to a widely held perception, the problem is not one of historical development or evolution, simply because European, or non-Muslim, societies have gone through it. Rather it is peculiar to an ideological faith, tied to temporal power which it cannot share with others not of the same faith.

All the same, one must consider the perfectly logical argument that, once the *sharia* becomes the sole basis of public order in these societies, non-Muslims must accept it as the law of the land with whatever disabilities it may impose upon them. One must also accept the fact that, in such an order, pluralism is not an option or a possibility. Whether such an order can be constructed (or restored) in any of these societies is, of course, another matter, and largely one of speculation.[56] The one instance where it has — Iran — requires no further comment.

In this connection, it is also fair to point to the relentless struggle between governments in the Middle East, as for example in Egypt, and those who call for their overthrow as usurpers, tyrants and infidels. In Egypt, it is a conflict between a basically secular state authority and those who deny its legitimacy because it refuses to establish a purely Islamic order. Yet the conflict is characterized by the hesitation of state authority to impose a functioning, institutionalized secular system. Such hesitation accentuates the problems of ethnicity and pluralism. Moreover, the state itself has tended to impose its own political uniformity that is in effect a practical denial of pluralism. So long as advocates of Islam insist that there is a specific Islamic political order, they will always challenge the authority of any order not based on the tenets of the faith.

Finally, the so-called Balkanization of the region on the basis of ethnic-sectarian autonomy is impractical and bloody. The only two alternatives are for the political accommodation of ethnicity in integrated secular political orders based on the nation-state, or the acceptance by minorities of tolerated and protected status in mainly Islamic societies under the rule of the *sharia*.

6

Islam and Europe: Conflict or Cooperation?

The Mediterranean basin is one of the oldest nuclear areas of human settlement and civilization. Similarly, it is one of the oldest routes for the movement of human habitation, the transport of people and goods. It is also one of the oldest centres in the meeting and confrontation — peaceful and hostile — between different peoples, cultures, civilizations, states and empires. Historically-decisive clashes between rival races and cultures, as well as between different religions, took place within its confines: Persians versus Greeks, Romans against Asians and Africans, Muslims against Christians, barbarians and vandals against settled societies and civilizations. It was from the Mediterranean that Greeks ventured to colonize the coast of Western Asia Minor a thousand years before the Christian era, or to settle the Cyrenaican coast and Egyptian Delta, Sicily and parts of southern Italy. Alexander the Great conquered the Levant and Egypt, the whole of Asia Minor and reached far into the Asian subcontinent to Transoxania and India. Clearly, the early period was dominated by the eastern Mediterranean with its classical Hellenic, Hellenistic, Roman and later Christian thrust. The western Mediterranean remained in obscurity at least until the eighth century AD and, as far as its European side is concerned, until well into the twelfth century.

A historical feature of the Mediterranean has been its migrations and shifting political arrangements: Egyptian, Athenian, Roman (including Byzantine), Arab-Islamic, Mongol and Ottoman. The colonization of the Greeks and the imperialism of the Romans were dynamic. They illustrated the natural perennial struggle over feeding places and natural resources. Thus the possession in ancient times of the rich Nile Valley and the Euphrates (Mesopotamia) was always coveted by conquering hordes. At the height of the Athenian maritime empire, one thousand cities paid tribute to it. The Carthaginian empire in North Africa, southern Spain, Corsica, Sardinia and southern Sicily was a trading state that acquired its wealth from subject provinces. The Roman Empire, which extended from the sands of Arabia to the snows of Scotland, was in a constant search for defensible frontiers. Then Rome itself succumbed to the Gothic hordes, and for 200 years the civilized Mediterranean world was at the mercy of migratory Teutons. Subsequently, feudal warlords in Europe fought against one another for a thousand years while the Arab and the Turkish Muslims dominated the Mediterranean. Occasionally, these European warlords united against the marauding Muslims. Out of this struggle emerged the Spanish, Portuguese, French, Dutch and English maritime powers. In the meantime, throughout the Middle Ages, trade and traffic in the luxuries of the Orient enriched Muslim and Italian merchants. In the sixteenth century, for instance, the English under Queen Elizabeth I launched the Levant Company to compete in commerce in the East against the Italian monopoly.

What links the lands of the eastern Mediterranean to those of the western Mediterranean is not merely the incontestable fact of early and continuous civilizational influences emanating primarily from the East. Despite the commercial and agricultural developments brought by the Phoenecians, say, in Tunisia and Tripolitania, the colonization of the Greeks and the imperial dominion of the Romans, it was the explosion of the conquering Muslim Arabs from Egypt and the Fertile Crescent that left its lasting impact: it gave the people of North Africa, for example, a new religion, Islam, and a new language, Arabic. A different and stronger link was forged by the Arab Islamic conquest; a new relationship was permanently established. Yet the link never led to a fusion, and the religious-linguistic affinity failed to produce the same social and political morphology in the Arab West of the western Mediterranean as is in the Arab East. In fact, in the thousand years that have since elapsed, the link between the two halves of the Arab, or Muslim, world has become a weak one, and the relationship between them tenuous and often abrasive.

The above case illustrates an interesting feature of the Mediterranean. Despite the proximity of different religions, cultures and civilizations, diversity remains paramount. Different societies at disparate levels of social and economic development coexist in a vast mosaic or, if you wish, a kaleidoscope. Even at the height of the Hellenistic period and its imperial Roman political expression, fusion was difficult. The Jews, for example, rejected integration into the Roman cultural norm. What kept the mosaic from shattering, or erupting into pandemoniacal conflict, was the long succession of powerful empires: Alexandrine, Roman, Byzantine, Islamic, Ottoman and European. The end of empire in this century rendered the mosaic problematic and — in some instances — very difficult to manage.

What is worthy of note is the fact that the Ottoman military thrust into the Balkans and Europe affected only the eastern Mediterranean. It hardly left a cultural-civilizational imprint. More interesting, however, was the earlier military incursion of the Arab Islamic empire into southern Italy and the Iberian Peninsula. That did have a cultural impact related to the earliest transmission of classical Greek thought and Aristotelian science into an awakening Europe between the ninth and thirteenth centuries. The clash between a Christian Europe during the Crusades and a declining, fragmented Islamic dominion further accelerated this process, most of it centred in the Mediterranean and increasingly in Italy, or the Italian city-states. One has simply to refer to the rising historical-political school of thought in Italy which was dazzled by the model from the east referred to as the 'vita tamerlani', culminating in Marsiglio and Machiavelli, or further afield the Paris School of Thomas Aquinas, and the rise of medical schools such as the one in Salerno.

Yet the explosion of scientific discovery in Europe later on (Newton, Copernicus, Kepler, Galileo) was due to a different Mediterranean influence; namely, the revival of classical Greek thought, the serious questioning of Aristotelian science and its eventual overthrow and replacement by Newtonian science; and the Renaissance. At that juncture, the separation between the eastern, central and western Mediterranean occurred. In any case, the fusion of Mediterranean societies under the influence of Graeco-Roman culture and civilization up to the seventh century AD had been broken by the conquering religion of Islam. What old Rome had achieved through law and military administration in a Mediterranean empire was, by the eighth century AD, disintegrating or breaking up under the weakened and declining New Rome, or the Byzantine empire.

To some extent the European revival in the fourteenth–sixteenth centuries was due, in part, to the influence of Islamic science and the transmission of classical culture to Europe by the fleeing scholars of Byzantium. Whatever the cause, its culmination was the Renaissance, an experience in which only a part of the Mediterranean took part. The eastern and southern Mediterranean remained untouched and unaffected by it. To a great extent, this epochal event established the cultural division between East and West, North and South in the Mediterranean. It was accompanied, if not actually paralleled, by the appearance of the conquering Turks in the eastern Mediterranean, the Balkans, Asia Minor and the Middle East, as successors to the marauding, though transient, Mongols and Tartars, and as the standard-bearers and defenders of the Islamic faith, culture and political dominion. The Mediterranean was very much their arena and the focal point of their clash with a rising, more modern Christian Europe. Still, they traded with the Italian city-states. The clash, however, was one between a restless seafaring Europe in the Mediterranean and a land-oriented Islamic empire founded by soldiers who were once slaves on horses.

The first European imperial power, Spain, concentrated its expansionist activities and dominion in the New World to the far west. Similarly, the Dutch maritime power operated there as well as in the Far East. But the expansion of European maritime power and imperial dominion under the French and the British in the eighteenth and nineteenth centuries used not only the ocean, but also the Mediterranean. By the early nineteenth century, the struggle between England and France for the control of the Mediterranean and the routes to the East was on in earnest, ending in British domination for over a century, until it was challenged by fascist Italy in the 1930s. For the British, the Mediterranean became the route to India and the centre of defence against Russian expansion in the Near East, using such political crucibles as the declining Ottoman state, Egypt, the Levant and the national independence movements in the Balkans. They supported Greek independence in the 1820s; together with France, which by then was more or less in control of the western Mediterranean in North Africa, they forced the introduction of reform in the Ottoman state; they stopped the imperialist and expansionist designs of the Viceroy of Egypt in the Levant; they bought Cyprus in 1876 as an outpost against Russian threats in the Mediterranean, and Khedive Ismail's Suez Canal shares as a means of controlling the new canal or waterway linking the Red Sea and Indian Ocean with the Mediterranean and Atlantic; and they occupied Egypt in 1882 for the same strategic reasons and soon came to control its hinterland up the Nile, to the Sudan and other parts.

The Mediterranean has also been the main route for the transmission of modern technology and new social and political ideas to its southern and eastern littoral. As European economic and military encroachments upon the Ottoman empire and its provinces proceeded apace from the eighteenth to the twentieth centuries, from the Napoleonic expedition to Egypt in 1798 to the British occupation of that country in 1882, it was inevitable that the societies of these areas would borrow, emulate and adapt European ideas and techniques in their economic, political and cultural spheres of activity. But their political reaction was also inevitable. It was one of rejection, at first couched in apologetic religious-civilizational terms of the dominant faith, Islam, such as Islamic reform, pan-Islamic movements, and the like. To this extent, this was a hostile reaction against the encroachments of Christian European power which was seen as representing an alien infidel civilization. Nevertheless, the independence movements, which were the other aspect of their reaction to Europe, took secular form, borrowing the ideas of European nationalism, expressed in the independent territorial nation-state. Thus the Atatürk episode in Turkey after the Great War, the Arab nationalist movement and the subsequent independence movements from the Levant and Egypt to North Africa, and Zionism among the Jews in Palestine; in short, what has been described as the decolonization process.

The process however was preceded by a series of clashes between west European and European Mediterranean powers on one side and a dying Ottoman state on the other: the succession of Russian wars with Turkey from the seventeenth to the nineteenth centuries and the Italian–Turkish War in Libya. In a sense, these were a reflection and manifestation of the role of the Mediterranean in the heightened European imperial scramble from the 1870s to the Great War. In fact, during both world wars, the Mediterranean was a major theatre of war. In the Great War the Ottoman state's belligerency on the side of the central powers meant that the contest was between it, as the major power in the eastern Mediterranean, and imperial Britain astride the Suez Canal, the Red and Arabian seas and further east. The campaigns in Iraq, Syria and Egypt brought an end to the Ottoman empire and the partition of the spoils by the victorious Entente powers in the East. This led to the creation of successor states under the respective spheres of influence of Britain and France, and thus the further complication of Mediterranean politics.

Similarly, during the Second World War the Mediterranean became the strategic fulcrum of the Allies; firstly, against the Axis's push to the East (the Libyan and North African campaigns, Iraq and Greece), and secondly, for springing back to Europe. In both instances the Mediterranean played a crucial role in the fortune of both Europeans and non-Europeans. Today, the strategic importance of the Mediterranean in the continuing East-West struggle is manifest in the significance attached to it by the superpowers. There is a difference, however. The Mediterranean has acquired its own regional/local importance as a contested area, not only between East and West, but also between North and South. There are local confrontations, contests and disputes: Greece and Turkey, Spain and Britain, the Arabs and Israel, among others. It has become a centre of terrorist activities and local, or regional, wars. There is an economic conflict, if only in the disparity between oil-producer and oil-consumer or between developed and less developed states, between those which are clearly aligned with major military-political-cultural blocs (e.g. NATO, the EEC, the Arab League) and those which are not.

More recently, as a result of what is generally referred to as Islamic militancy, or political Islam, and events in the volatile Middle East, there has been a renewed Islamic-Western (Christian) confrontation, a clash of cultures, with the Mediterranean as one of its venues and potential arenas. Essentially, the contest is about power. Muslims believe that Europe, or the West, has undermined Islamic cultural identity through political, economic and military domination. They believe further that God enjoins Muslims to control temporal power in order to realize His pattern for the world. The predomination of a modern industrial civilization and culture that is basically of European provenance is thus viewed as infidel and harmful and, to this extent, it is rejected. Now that they have the economic means, Muslims contend they must assert their will and project their power abroad, including in the Mediterranean. A corollary of this is the spilling over of internecine conflict from the southern to the northern shores of the Mediterranean, and the exertion of pressure on the domestic and external policies of the countries involved.

As always, then, the Mediterranean remains a venue and an arena of all these competing interests and clashing cultures, reflecting differences in religious belief, cultural orientation, and economic and political interests. Politically, the Mediterranean remains a passage, a locus of battle, a route to somewhere. There has been — at least in the recent past — European Mediterranean policy, imperial Mediterranean policy, Muslim policy, and today, superpower policy regarding the lands and seas between Suez and Gibraltar, Suez and the Dardanelles. One can easily enumerate all the states possessing Mediterranean territory. The question, though, is which among them can have a so-called Mediterranean policy. The British did in the nineteenth and early twentieth centuries, and the Italians did earlier in this century, primarily because the Mediterranean has always been a main artery of empire. French interest in the Mediterranean was related to their position in Europe, especially *vis-à-vis* Germany, and mainly in the western Mediterranean. Italy always needed and still needs Mediterranean allies. Turkey and Greece remain important in this connection. Today it is a vital air and sea route, highly vulnerable to air, submarine and land-based missile attack.

So what major forces are at work in the Mediterranean today? Clearly NATO and the EEC, the latter comprising at least four Christian Mediterranean powers. So are the superpowers. The geopolitical and strategic issues remain Cyprus, the Greek-Turkish confrontation in the Aegean, the transport of energy supplies, local trouble in North Africa, the future of Gibraltar, terrorism — most of it emanating recently from the lands of Islam — and the so-called North–South dichotomy.[1] In the latter are featured the volatile political conditions of the Middle East, comprising the Arab–Israel conflict, Islamic militancy, and civil and other regional wars, all of which highlight the problems of domestic instability, regional security and terrorism.

It is important to note that only during the Hellenic and Hellenistic, or Graeco-Roman, periods of hegemony was there anything like a 'Mediterranean civilization'. With the appearance of the Muslim Arabs and Turks this uniform civilization was transformed, if not in fact destroyed, and soon bifurcated into a Western-Christian and an Oriental-Muslim one. To a great extent, this division occurred earlier. Although the earlier Muslim Arabs (seventh–tenth centuries) seemed to accept Greek rational philosophy, the very same rationalism was finally and irrevocably rejected with the consecration of Islamic orthodoxy in the thirteenth and fourteen centuries. There is, then, not one civilization in the Mediterranean but several. In fact, there is no such thing as a 'Mediterranean civilization'. But is there a shared, or common, 'Mediterranean culture'? This is an arguable proposition. In reality, what one observes in the Mediterranean is a great diversity of ethnic groups, religious communities, and cultural norms. There is also a great disparity in economic conditions and activity, and serious differences in social organization and political arrangements. This diversity and all of these differences and disparities constitute sources, levels and areas of actual and potential conflict, as well as of cooperation. Thus Italy, France, Greece and Spain partake of a Mediterranean geographical presence, a relatively common historical and cultural experience. At the same time, they are full members of the West European–North Atlantic military alliance and a European Economic Community.

On the other side of the Mediterranean, several countries and states are members of different linguistic, national-religious, cultural and political regional arrangements: the Arab League, the Islamic Conference Organization, the Organization of African Unity, the Afro–Asian Solidarity Conference and other such organizations. In fact, the religious-cultural differences between the two sides of the Mediterranean are manifested today in several ways: institutional, societal and political. Beyond the eastern and southern Mediterranean one comes across military and theocratic autocracies, sectarian fortress regimes, tribal chieftaincies, religious nationalisms, militant religious movements, dynastic autocracies and single-party states. Religion still takes precedence over national-territorial identity and jurisdiction. There is an official religion of the state and a minimum of an integrated secular national community. On the whole, the principle of the territorial nation-state is not firmly established, and authority is tenuous. Similarly, authoritarianism and autocracy, violent as opposed to deliberative politics, are the norm rather than the exception. The idea of tolerating opposition has yet to take root. While there are states in these parts of the Mediterranean, there are hardly any nation-states.

One can document the above-listed features by looking at any of the Levant States — Syria, Lebanon, Jordan and Iraq — or the North African states of Tunisia, Morocco and, to a lesser extent or degree, Algeria and Egypt. A commonly agreed-upon fundamental principle for the organization of political power — i.e. the establishment of a political order — has yet to be found in these societies. One of the obstacles to this development has been the clash between religion, with its extensive cultural complex or ethos, and secular modernity under which the national secular state arose. Another has been the disparity in economic development. A third has been the nature of authority, the perception of rule and the concept of the public interest or common good. The close personal — and personalized — relation between the ruler and ruled, or the state, is due in part to the lack of an abstract concept of the corporate personality. The body politic, or the public, cannot be conceived separately from its individual, physical component parts. Similarly, whereas in the European Mediterranean there is a concept of natural law, it does not exist in the non-European Mediterranean. Consequently, such matters as individual rights deriving from this higher law in order to protect the individual from the excesses of the state are difficult to formulate and maintain. Rather, individual rights derive from one's religious identity or faith, especially when God and nature are one.

The unwillingness in the non-European Mediterranean to tolerate opposition is related to the lack of scepticism and experimentation. Consequently, voluntary associations — public endeavour outside state-governmental functions and initiative — are at a premium. For the same reasons a ruler, so long as he is in office, concentrates power in his hands and personifies the state, public order — even morality. A corollary of this is the difficulty entailed in the problem of succession on an agreed premise of legitimacy. This was particularly the case with the various military rulers of the 1950s and 1960s. It also suggests a minimum of popular participation in public business or affairs, and the weakness of public and private institutions. Public power becomes difficult to limit or make accountable to representative bodies.

For these and other reasons, much of politics in these parts of the Mediterranean is a variant of religion, if not religion incarnate. In Lebanon, for instance, politics is religion incarnate. Because Lebanon failed since 1943 to construct a political regime outside religion it imploded into civil chaos, and disintegrated. This failure brought to the fore once again the problem of minorities, the challenge of state structures — even state boundaries — by armed groups seeking some kind of autonomy. At the same time it revived religious militancy which seeks power in order to establish God's word as law on earth. This kind of movement pervades the Levant, even Egypt. As we know, the nation-state is a political, not a legal concept. The state in Islam is an ideological concept. It exists in order to promote the faith and implement God's revealed law.

We have then in terms of religion, culture and politics at least two opposing trends — and realities — in the Mediterranean. These opposing trends and realities have, as I have tried to indicate, their historical roots and foundations. Even such common features as separatist movements are motivated by different factors on the two sides of the Mediterranean. Thus, surely, the Corsican separatists view themselves as a nation that is separate and distinct, or at least different, from metropolitan France. The same may be true of the Basque separatists in Spain. The Kurds may be the only similar, or parallel, case in Turkey, Iraq and Iran; that is, they are motivated by a sense of separate national community. The rest, Christian, Shii and others, base their demands for autonomy on religious faith.

Even Turkey, despite the achievements of its great laicist secularizer Atatürk, defies any Mediterranean description. Rather its republican epic between 1923 and today, if anything, has emphasized the Asiatic greatness of the nation and its antecedents. Of the Arab states, only Lebanon, before its disintegration and when it was still dominated by the political culture of the Christians deriving from their experience of autonomy in the Mountain over two centuries, claimed a Mediterranean identity of sorts. It was also true of the Egyptians throughout the 1930s, when their view of their Islamic–Arab connections was weak and even scornful: they prided themselves on belonging to a Mediterranean 'civilization'. They even deplored the break in their 'membership' in that civilization occasioned by the Arab and Turkish conquests of their country, i.e. the land-oriented Asiatics. For the rest, the

Mediterranean as a historical–cultural unit or identity tag is meaningless.

It is important to remember therefore that when dealing with the Mediterranean one is faced with a culturally and religiously highly diverse region. This diversity, moreover, manifests itself in very complex social, political and economic differences — and conflict. Ethnic-sectarian based conflicts proliferate just as national–religious ones do: Christians versus Muslims, Arabs versus Persians, Arabs versus Jews, Greeks versus Turks. But there is also the conflict between religious militants who demand a radical restoration of the past against secularists who wish to roll with modernity; between those who demand the fusion of sanctity and power against those who consider power to be basically mundane — and profane.

Alas, a large part of the Mediterranean has had no Marsiglio, no Machiavelli and no Galileo, not to mention others. When in the late eighteenth and early nineteenth centuries it was forced to face up to the challenge of modernity it did so under a succession of autocratic rulers, modernizing despots, who sought to borrow the trappings of modernity in order to increase their own power over their subjects at home and their adversaries abroad. For good or ill, in the southern Mediterranean the individual was never freed from the burden of tradition and the past, from the constraints of religion and religiously based or sanctioned authority.

It is perhaps interesting to speculate on the periodic appearance of strong men in the political evolution of states in the Mediterranean. This was the case in the European Mediterranean states in the 1920s and 1930s, and more so today in the case of the non-European ones. It is not therefore only the diversity of historical experience and cultural orientation that divide the northern from the southern Mediterranean. There is actually a gulf or chasm between the political culture currently prevailing in the south and that more common among the societies in the north. Even in the more practical and mundane area of political orientation and affiliation there is a wide gap between the two sides of the Mediterranean. Even if such labels or terms are meaningless, Third World Socialism and so-called Nonalignment are political incantations that are common in the southern Mediterranean. Recently though, they seem to have found their way in at least one putatively European Mediterranean country, Greece.

In seeking cooperation or confrontation in the Mediterranean, European countries in the region must recognize the long-standing historical, cultural and religious differences between them and the non-European countries involved. The latter, in fact, will approach any such attempts at cooperation with these differences very much in their minds and in the forefront of their policy considerations.

The energy crisis of October 1973 arose almost completely from economic and political conditions prevailing outside Europe. It was due largely to the Middle East conflict and the involvement of the superpowers in it. Yet Western Europe comprised the group of industrial countries most vulnerable to the crisis in energy supplies and the sharp rise in their price. Partly this was due to the fact that since the Second World War, Western European nations had run down their coal-mining industries in the face of available abundant and cheap supplies of oil from the Middle East. The post-war manufacturing and trade boom experienced by these countries led to an ever-higher consumption of Middle Eastern oil and a near total dependence on it. When the reduction in the production and the increase in the price of that commodity occurred almost simultaneously, the vulnerability of these countries led them to the edge of panic.

Europe's helplessness in influencing the outcome of the Middle East conflict added to their predicament, especially when the oil weapon was used by the Arab exporters as an instrument of political coercion. Not only was there a fundamental shift in the energy position where Europe was concerned after the war, but the shift in the balance of military power as regards the Middle East from Europe to the United States and the Soviet Union compounded the difficulty. In the 1960s and 1970s, in addition to the superpowers, Iran and Egypt in the Middle East were acquiring relatively greater military strength. Europe, incidentally, had given up this kind of national aim or path long ago, and more readily so — perhaps with undue abandon — when its advanced industrial societies opted for more elaborate public services and welfare benefits for their members. Then, coming at a time of deceleration in industrial growth, inflation and monetary difficulties, the 1973 energy crisis looked like a major turning point in the international redistribution of wealth (i.e. economic strength) and, possibly, political power.

That a transfer of wealth was taking place on an unprecedented scale from the developed industrial nations to the underdeveloped oil-exporting ones cannot be gainsaid. The transfer, at first, was one of financial assets, but soon also — ominously for the industrial nations — one of real resources since, with their astronomical accumulation of financial assets, oil-exporting countries began to buy into the substantial resources of the developed countries. They appeared to have the ability to buy the goods and industries of other nations.

More intricate was the capacity of this newly acquired purchasing power to influence the industrial world in general, and to buy the political support of the more vulnerable industrial states for certain issues in particular. The combination of an essential raw material and a money weapon appeared formidable and threatened to undermine, if not actually overthrow, the 'political world' and 'international order' so painstakingly and precariously constructed largely by the West from Vienna to Versailles to San Francisco and Dunbarton Oaks. For a time, it had thrown it into disarray.

Soon there were indications of 'alliances' and alignments based on new perceptions of common economic–political interests among the so-called Third World countries, or the less developed world against the industrial West, i.e. Europe, the United States and, on its periphery, Japan. One even detected the savouring of a demonstration of newly found power (regardless of how real or imagined it may have been) by the Muslim Arab states. Psychologically, this constituted an important fillip to their pride and dignity, particularly since it could be demonstrated and used against their erstwhile Western or European political masters. Inevitably, whatever its manifestations, this sense of and claim to power reflected a deep-seated resentment and, in some cases, hostility towards the Western European world.

After all, the concept of the 'international order' and that of the comity of nations was essentially a European one. The rules, conventions and customs regulating its operation were devised almost exclusively by Europeans. At certain times, Muslim Arabs found it an intolerable order, unjust and unfriendly. There was no reason why they should be culturally or morally bound by it, loyal to it, or committed to its perpetuation. In fact, one could argue that, in terms of cultural tradition and intellectual outlook, it was an order inspired by a Christian civilizational nexus.

On the other hand, the newly rich Muslim Arab states realized that their wealth which would inevitably have an impact upon their societies in terms of industrial development and economic diversification, pre-supposed, indeed dictated, their greater interdependence with the rest of the international economic order of which Europe, the West, is an important integral part, if not its very core. Economically speaking, therefore, the interest of the new rich oil-exporting countries to cooperate with it was clear and straightforward. The dilemma arose over political issues or confrontations, so that the choice of whether to be for that essentially European–Western international order, or against it, was not as easy to make.

It is elementary to observe that, given their new wealth — which under certain conditions could have been translated into political power — the Muslim Arabs demanded recognition by the traditional great powers as equal partners in the operation at least of the so-called international economic system. By 1974 they possessed the kind of political leverage that seemed to elevate their international status. At the same time, their massive investments in Europe and the United States rendered them vitally interested in, if not plainly dependent on, the maintenance of an international system largely devised and operated exclusively by these great powers.

Surely though, new and successive Muslim government elites were expected to gain not only greater proficiency, but also self-confidence, after a long period — nearly 200 years — of a humiliating experience, during which Europe had exercised economic and political power over them. They also felt that they would gain strength with a larger role in the management of regional and international affairs.

In the face of these developments, Europe felt that most if not all of her economic and security assumptions were endangered, if not already overtaken by events. There was uncertainty and disarray both within European ranks and in the relationship of Europe with the superpowers in the age of detente. The joltingly rapid rise in the bargaining power of the Muslim oil-exporting countries on which Europe depended for its energy supplies rendered the Western European nations, in the circumstances, most susceptible to political coercion and blackmail.

If this brief, captious description of the energy crisis, or the confrontation between oil-producers and consumers a decade ago, is reasonable, one could approach the question of cultural attitudes and national perceptions (bearing in mind the level of interdependence imposed by the forces of the international economic system), not so much from the perspective of what unites Europe and the Islamic Middle East, but from that of what divides and separates them; not from the facile premise that all men everywhere are the same, share similar passions, suffer uniform weaknesses and face identical problems, but from that of the reality that they often *desire different things*, harbour disparate, diametrically opposed *aims*, are formed and conditioned by sharply diverse cultural traditions and intellectual outlooks, which include different beliefs, attitudes, values, prejudices and perceptions.

I shall emphasize why and how Europe differs from the Islamic Middle East, even though ever since *humanitas* was first uttered by pre-Christian and Christian European philosophers the assumption has been that an ecumenical (hopelessly ideological) culture and universal polity were possible; even though Western social scientists in the last thirty years tried, on the basis of muddled single-conception universal theories of 'science', to construct a notion of a linear progression from the 'hell' of underdevelopment to the Western 'paradise' of development, implying a future universe of political uniformity.

I shall also make a few remarks regarding a European observation of how the Arabs perceived their October 1973 'achievement' in war and new economic power, which was to provide them with political influence far beyond their region, and wholly disproportionate to their other societal or national strength.

We can, at the outset, agree on the assertion regarding the importance of religions in the development of civilizations. And when we speak of Europe and the perceptions of Europeans, we inevitably imply a cultural tradition and intellectual outlook that were, for good or ill, influenced, if not actually formed, by Christianity. Similarly, when we speak of an Arab Middle East, or an Arab World, we recognize that at its base, its heart, lies the religion and culture of Islam. One may well go no further by resorting to the common cliché concerning the kinship or similarity — the common origins, as they say — of the three great monotheistic religions of Judaism, Christianity and Islam. The point though is that certain things happened to, were undertaken and accomplished by Christianity *in Europe*, which never occurred in Islam; indeed, which Islam never experienced. It was these developments — some conscious and deliberate, others inadvertent and accidental — and experiences which cumulatively produced the differences in intellectual formation, cultural attitudes, economic, social and political perceptions between Europe and Islam.

The philosophers among us might wish to make the separation 500 years before the Christian era, when the strange Greeks, particularly the Athenians, began to create an original political culture which represented a break, an evolutionary mutation or take-off, from the civilizations of the East — Persia, Mesopotamia and the Nile Valley. They introduced a new type and style of thinking about man and the universe. For example, they distinguished between man as a natural, ethical and moral being on the one hand, and man as a political being, a citizen of a man-made political order on the other. They formulated the idea of the state as a supreme community of *citizens*, whose relations were regulated by law, and the purpose of which was justice. They suggested the earliest definition of law as 'an ordinance of human reason for the common good'. They drew the earliest distinction between legitimate authority and tyrannical power, and commented on the psychological, economic, social and political foundations of human behaviour and the causes of its deviation or degeneration; that is, of its change. In short, they founded a political philosophy based on man's reason, and asserted that 'a man who remains outside the *polis* is either a god or a beast'. They gave the natural and political order a dynamic, a developmental and teleological dimension in contrast to a statically conceived one. They tried to transform man from a worshipping, genuflecting *subject* of a despot, emperor, god-king or whatever, to a free, participating *citizen* under the law.

This classical political vision of man, however, had no universalist pretensions, and the achievement, if indeed it was one, suffered great difficulties. It was limited and culturally exclusive. It was technologically deficient, even inept. The experiment among the querulous Greeks was bitter and short-lived; after a disastrous civil war, it was overwhelmed by conquest, leading to a more ecumenical re-fusion of the Eastern and Western worlds astride the Mediterranean under the strange genius of Alexander.

From the Greeks to the Renaissance, however, there was a kind of socio-genetic continuity in the evolution of Europe regarding the problems of political order and the main concerns of law and government. As far as Europe is concerned — in fact the West as a whole — the political ideas and cultural attitudes which linger today were born in the Middle Ages: democracy, sovereignty, political authority, law and justice. Christianity played a decisive formative role even though our present age is not one of religious faith. Contemporary political ideas and institutions are firmly embedded in this historical experience of one thousand years. Thus the very concept of the modern state as an autonomous body of citizens with its own laws is originally a thirteenth-century idea. Politics after that time came to deal with the problem of the ultimate authority of government to lay down the means and ends of a society, organized into a political community. The whole political debate from the Middle Ages, the Renaissance and the Reformation to the English, American, French and Russian revolutions has been essentially over the problem of where original authority lies and who has the right to legislate. Needless to say, the revived impact of pre-Christian classical (i.e. Aristotelian) ideas via Thomas Aquinas, Marsilio of Padua and others was made even more effective by a long spell of medieval populism in town and country in the form of popular uprisings, peasant revolts, heretical sects, etc. There are even those who view the role of the Crusades — the source of such long-felt resentment and antagonism between Islam and Christendom — as large-scale movements of the masses.

The explosion of individualism, a sense of history (the so-called rediscovery of antiquity) in the Renaissance, laid the foundations of politics as an autonomous human activity, free from the considerations or encumbrances of religion, and heralded the rise of the European variant of nationalism.

The separation of hierarchical orders into natural and supranatural, temporal and spiritual, made possible the separation of political man from spiritual (religious) man. The link, so to speak, between God and nature was cut. Positive, man-made, enforceable law, deriving in part from a higher natural law, not revealed by a deity or its divine intermediaries, rendered a human community not only one of 'believers', but primarily one of citizens. Soon the notion of contract in the establishment of a political relationship, implying a legal bond for the member inside the community, made possible such ideas as consent and representation.

Men of the Renaissance assumed that man's passions were neither good nor bad, only necessary, thus introducing the relatively modern sense of individual responsibility. For the first time, perhaps, the relevance of providence to human freedom and necessity, as expressed for example in Dante's insistence on man's moral responsibility, released man to reflect freely on the great issues independently of religion if not in opposition to its institutional authorities. Rationalism and historical enquiry became the hallmarks of a new 'worldliness', characterized in turn by scepticism and systematic questioning. Formal, typical notions of sin and salvation receded into the background; religion became a matter of personal feeling or belief and individual conscience.

This release of European man from formal, structured Christianity reestablished him as the pivot of civic life, capable of (or at least arrogantly believing he was capable of) mastering and shaping his own fate or destiny. The body politic became autonomous, not merely the adjunct or auxiliary of some spiritual, religious order of things. The passive, static *via contemplativa* of traditional, formal Christianity was no longer considered adequate to serve or defend the state. The latter needed enforceable laws, not unenforceable morals.

Later, progress in science and the eventual dethronement of 'King Aristotle' by Newton, Galileo and Copernicus rendered man and his environment or universe as natural physical and biological objects of investigation, observation and experimentation. The world, in fact, came to be viewed by the European as a rather finite physical and moral cosmos. It is in these senses perhaps that the Renaissance may be considered the harbinger, if not founder, of the modern European age.

The explosion of a 'print civilization' after 1500, along with scientific and other developments, brought along ideas of Europe's mission, conveniently complementing the rise of its technological, commercial and military power. The old Crusades, with the ignorant rantings of its propagandists and publicists against the world of Islam, elicited the Muslim response of *jihad* (Holy War) against the infidels. Now, the economic, military and political penetration of the Muslim East by a renascent Europe provided the basis of empire in the name of 'progress'. It is the world order established by these events that is being finally challenged now, by an opposing world, holding different attitudes regarding what constitutes the public or common good, the nature of wealth, knowledge, and the state. Thus, notions of political freedom are not held in common — in fact they are alien to Islam.

Yet in spite of the European penetration into Islamic lands, the old distorted writings of the divines about Muslims so common among Byzantine, Crusader and even later European utterances, gave way, as of the 18th century, to the European study of Islam and the Muslims for their own sake, without however a corresponding gesture on the part of the Muslims. None the less there persisted among professional European intellectuals a tendency to see the Islamic world through the distorting glass of essentially European categories of thought and language.

Alas, for good or ill, at the core of every community, political order, and culture or civilization, there is a body of shared beliefs, attitudes and, importantly, myths. This is a universal tendency in man to seek a meta-historical dimension to his life in order to assuage the bitter reality of his finite existence. Whereas in Islam, theoretically at least, the core myth underlying its Weltanschauung, its view and perception of *the other*, is rejectionist, therefore abrasive and uncompromising in its universalist teleology, developments in Europe (without any value judgement about their quality) have been such as to transcend this dichotomy in perception. Accommodation of *the other* became possible (granted, not always successfully, peacefully or gracefully) by the formulation and embodiment in law of such notions as citizenship and political toleration. So far, it has not necessarily looked at the non-European parts of the world in the antithetical terms of 'we versus them', whereas, often for a variety of reasons, the Muslim Arab has.

The imperial civil servant's stereotype of the 'native' — Muslim, Arab or other — was long demolished and abandoned by the Europeans themselves before the empires were disbanded or disintegrated under the pressure of events and opposition. To this extent, the Muslim perhaps perceives the European not only as a past aggressor, but as a permanent enemy, an infidel outside the pale. Similarly, and to this extent, the exclusiveness of Islam as translated into political reality even in present day state structures prevents it from dealing with the European in any relationship other than a temporary one (e.g. guest), but never as a fully fledged member of the political community short of conversion. The European, therefore, harbours a fear and feels some apprehension about the possible conjoining by the Muslim of wealth and force in the pursuit of prestige and power for the dignity of the Community of Believers.

The European observes today that, in partaking of a common Islamic heritage (which incidentally remains at the heart of such movements as Arab nationalism), with its universalist pretensions and past confrontations with the non-Islamic world, Arab rulers and states, as well as individuals, perceive their collective interest in terms of the solidarity of the Community of Believers and its struggle for prestige and power *vis-à-vis* the outside world. The tensions that the Muslims experience in their relations with the non-Muslim world and their feeling of alienation from it will continue to influence their response to events. Stated more simply, they are committed to a different scale of values, virtues and ethic, regardless of the imported secular rationalizations they may adumbrate for that commitment.

One thus detects in recent Arabic writing at least, and particularly in statements by Arab officials for home consumption, a resentment of all the past real and imagined ills and injustices visited by the West, from the Crusaders to the nineteenth century imperialists, upon Muslim Arab society. There is in these utterances a sharp tone of defiance and an allusion to revenge, which project the 'Arab restoration' at hand. In short, the Islamic euphoria and new psychology of confrontation with an alien world that has kept, say, 'Arab genius' down, provide still further sources of friction and misunderstanding.

Historically, the European world and the Islamic world have experienced two types of relationship: one of confrontation from the eighth to the nineteenth centuries, and one of European domination and Islamic subjugation in the twentieth. They never experienced a relationship of political interdependence which is probably the one needed now. In view of the ominous recrudescence today of violent conflict between ethnic and sectarian-based 'nationalisms' — Cyprus, Greece and Turkey, Iraq, Lebanon — one could envisage the beginning of an era of religious wars. In black moments of despair, one could easily feel like medieval man, waiting for the 'bang' if he is faithless, or the Second Coming if he is a believer.

Perhaps one ought to sharpen the controversy in the debate by suggesting that these religious-cultural based differences between Europe and the Muslim Arab world could conceivably lead to a new historical round of clash and confrontation. The story of the decline, if not destruction of British industrial capabilities, imperceptibly at first in the late nineteenth century with the export of capital and technology (for purposes of cheaper costs and maximum profits) to distant parts of the empire, ultimately meant the exportation, or transfer, of manufacturing abilities. There is no reason, given the international shift or redistribution in wealth of the last decade, why this should not happen again to many more European nations.

One need hardly be reminded that fear and antagonism between cultures and civilizations are usually transmitted from generation to generation. Stereotypes, cultural attitudes and national perceptions may decline, recede, change, even disappear among a very small elite in any national group. Whether this can also occur on a mass scale is another matter. So long as different cultures or civilizations do not share a minimum core of common fundamental values — that is, so long as they do not have a certain commonality of perceptions and interests — the reformulation and re-casting of their relations under new conditions and novel circumstances is always a difficult, delicate and dangerous task.

One need not have Cleon's 'violent character' to appreciate the force of his remarks about once-subject peoples. Fear and conspiracy do play a part in the daily relation of men and states; leadership depends more often than not on superior strength rather than the goodwill of others; and people rebel when they have been badly treated. The European, surely, is vaguely aware of these aspects of a changing relationship with another culture, to which great prosperity has come suddenly and unexpectedly in a matter of a few years. And this, in any culture, breeds arrogance.

The European views the Arab Middle East primarily as the major source of his energy supplies and therefore as being important to his economic well-being and national security. He also wishes clearly to maintain and perpetuate the international order originally founded and developed by Europeans. At the same time, without recourse to myths or stereotypes, he recognizes that the value-laden civilizational foundation of this order is alien to the average Muslim or Arab, and is uncertain about the latter's attitude to it in the event he gains the upper political hand. He is also embarrassingly aware of the Muslim's resentment and, in cases, hostility that derives from his past experience of subjugation to Europe. Above all, if he also happens to be a Protestant, the European carries in his psyche a sense of guilt towards the Muslim, particularly when the Muslim Arab fuses in his mind the role of the European in the establishment of Israel. It is clearly difficult for the Muslim to accept a sovereign political entity in his cultural–geographical region — the *dar al-islam* — that is so alien, so Jewish.

Islam, the European feels, has been a *political* religion from its inception. It conquered an empire in the name of Allah and His Prophet. Political acts therefore are theoretically performed or undertaken for the glory of Allah. To this extent, Islam has never had to face the so-called problem of secularism, since the faith itself entailed a political duty or obligation on the part of the believer. War, for the Muslim, whatever its purpose, when engaged in against non-Muslims is, by definition, a Holy War in the cause of Islam. There are, for example, those among the Muslims who pride themselves on the fact that Muslims have not signed a treaty with infidels in several centuries. (Needless to say, the Turks have many times.) This reference to pseudo-history reflects an attitude and a perception of no mean significance.

In contemplating, therefore, future chances and patterns of interdependence, the European observes that the earliest carriers of the Islamic message, the tribes (settled or nomadic) have left their imprint of a *tribal ethos* on most Muslim Arab societies, whether in town or country. In the determination of relations between men, even groups, dominance rather than cooperation seems to be the foremost and primary objective. This is especially true in hierarchical relationships. Surely, such attitudes and perceptions are of the essence in any projections of interdependence.

Notes

INTRODUCTION

1. 'The chief purpose of the Patten Foundation . . . is to bring to the campus lecturers of eminence who will be in residence at the University for at least two months.' Under the terms of the bequest, which became available upon the death of Mr Patten (3 May 1936), there is chosen each year a distinguished professor who is in residence for one semester or a part of a semester. Additional funds are used to invite Patten lecturers, who are on campus for a shorter period of time and are asked to deliver one or two public lectures.

2. The third lecture was a critical bibliographical review of recent writing dealing with the so-called Islamic revolution. A version of that lecture was published as 'The Rise of the Clerisocracy', *Encounter* (London), vol. 58, no. 3 (March 1982), pp. 68–76, and reprinted in P.J. Vatikiotis, *Arab and Regional Politics in the Middle East*, London and New York, 1984, pp. 60–76.

3. Cambridge, 1965. Very briefly, his thesis was that there were several states in which the societies are Muslim, but no Islamic states in the strict Islamic legal-juridical or theological sense.

4. Princeton, 1957.

5. Chicago, 1947.

6. M. Iqbal, *Reconstruction of Religious Thought*, Oxford, 1938.

7. See, for example, Ali Hillal Dessouki (ed.), *Islamic Resurgence in the Arab World*, New York, 1982; A.S. Cudsi and Ali Hillal Dessouki (eds.), *Islam and Power*, London, 1980; Edward Mortimer, *Faith and Power: The Politics of Islam*, New York, 1982; Shaul Bakhash, *The Reign of the Ayatollahs: Iran and the Islamic Revolution*, New York, 1985; Daniel Pipes, *In the Path of God: Islam and Political Power*, New York, 1983; John L. Esposito (ed.), *Islam and Development: Religion and Sociopolitical Change*, Syracuse, 1980; Martin Kramer, *Political Islam*, Beverley Hills, 1980; John Osbert Voll, *Islam: Continuity and Change in the Modern World*, Boulder, Colorado, 1982; and several others.

8. The full title of the first volume is *Dalil al-muslim al-hazin li muqtada al-suluk fi'l- qarn al-ʿishrin*.

9. See especially his *al-Muslimun wa'l-aqbat fi itar al-jamaʿa al-wataniyya*, Beirut, 1980.

10. P. J. Vatikiotis, *The Fatimid Theory of the State*, Lahore, 1957.

11. See Chapter 6.

12. Two devastating European/world wars in 25 years; scarce and rapidly depleting world resources requiring global economic and related planning; in effect, an interdependent economic world order developing while politically states remain stubbornly parochial, divided and fragmented on the basis of the jealously guarded notion of national sovereignty.

13. A relevant demographic projection in this connection is the estimate that in the year 2000 there will be 265 million people in the central land area of the Middle East (from Afghanistan to the Levant, and from Turkey to Egypt and the Gulf) who probably cannot be adequately fed by the less than four per cent of cultivable land area in the region. The vast majority (over 90 per cent) of these will be Muslim. Many of them will seek to go north and west (there are already 2 million Turks in Germany, nearly 2.5 million North Africans in France; about 300,000 Pakistanis in the UK; about 250,000 multi-national Muslims in Italy and Greece). It is thus estimated that by the end of the century 25 per cent of Europe's population will be Muslim. What is not clear is if this figure applies exclusively to Western Europe — specifically the EEC countries — or the whole of Europe. (The Soviet Union alone will have nearly 100 million Muslims in its constituent Asian republics.) In any case, the infusion of such a sizeable culturally exogenous element into Western European societies and their bodies politic is bound to affect their character and further evolution, while promoting, in the meantime, various forms of conflict and civil strife.

14. See Hamadi al-'Ubeidi, *al-Da'wa'l-islamiyya wa ẑuhur al-dawla*, Tunis, 1980; Muhammad Salim al-'Awwa, *Fi'l-nizam al-siyasi li'l-dawla al-islamiyya,* 4th edn., Cairo, 1980 (1st edn., 1975); Muhammad Jawad Mugnieh, *al-Khomeini wa al-dawla al-islamiyya*, Beirut, 1979; Sayyid Qutb, *Fi zilal al-qur'an,* 5th edn., 8 vols., Beirut, 1967 (also 1971); 'Abd al-Hamid Metwalli, *Azamat al-fikr al-siyasi al-islami fi al-'asr al-hadith*, Alexandria, 1970; Abdullah al-Nafisi, *'Indama yahkumu al-islam*, London, 1983.

15. See op. cit. Note in this connection the paradoxical though powerful role of Islam as the basis of nationalist opposition to secular state authorities, as in the case of the Central Asian Muslims in the Soviet Union against the Moscow (Christian–Marxist)-dominated political system. Cf. Alexandr Benningsen and Marie Broxup, *The Islamic Threat to the Soviet State*, London, 1982; Alexandr Benningsen, 'Official Islam and Sufi Brotherhoods in the Soviet Union Today', in A.S. Cudsi and A. Hillal Dessouki (eds), *Islam and Power,* London, 1981 (reprinted 1982), pp. 95–106. The same applies to the separatist movements among Muslim communities in the Philippines and Thailand.

16. See A.K.S. Lambton, *State and Government in Medieval Islam*, Cambridge, 1981.

17. Carleton Coon, *Caravan: The Story of the Middle East*, Philadelphia, 1953.

18. See Chapters 4 and 5. It may be noted that in 1932 the British mandate over Iraq was terminated and followed by a bilateral treaty after Iraq was proclaimed formally an independent nation-state and admitted to membership of the League of Nations. In 1936 the Anglo-Egyptian Treaty further diluted British control over the affairs of Egypt, allowing the latter a greater measure of independence as a nation-state. See Majid Khadduri, *Independent Iraq*, New York, 1960, and P.J. Vatikiotis, *History of Egypt*, 3rd ed., London, 1985.

19. See in this connection especially the writings of Abu al-Hasan al-Nadvi, *Madha khasira al-ʿalam bi-inhitat al-muslimin*, 8th edn., Kuwait, 1970 (1st edn. 1950), and *al-Tariq ila'l-saʿada wa'l-qiyada li'l-duwal wa'l-mujtama'at al-islamiyya al-hurra*, Beirut, 1982. The thrust of both of these works is based on the assertion that Islam is a religion of superiority (*din istiʿla'*) which therefore cannot and must not allow man to be governed in this world by non-Muslims. The author also exhibits in both works a serious lack of understanding of Western political culture and its values.

20. Barbara Tuchman, *The March of Folly*, London, 1984.

CHAPTER 1

1. See al-Ghazali, *Ihya' ʿulum al-din,* 4 vols., Cairo, 1928.
2. Cf. al-Mawardi, *al-Ahkam al-sultaniyya*, Cairo, 1909, and Ibn Taymiya, *al-Siyasa al-sharʿiyya*, Cairo, n.d. Further on Sunni political theory, see H.A.R. Gibb, *Studies on the Civilization of Islam,* edited by S.J. Shaw and W.R. Polk, Princeton, 1982, pp. 141–75. Cf. P.J. Vatikiotis, 'Authoritarianism and Autocracy in the Middle East', in *Arab and Regional Politics in the Middle East*, op. cit., pp. 135–51.
3. See P. Crone and M. Cook *Hagarism, the Making of the World of Islam*, Cambridge, 1977.
4. For example, Khomeini's references to America as Satan.
5. See G.E. von Grunebaum, *Medieval Islam*, Chicago, 1945.
6. P. Crone, *Slaves on Horses*, Cambridge, 1980.
7. Ibid.
8. Sura liv: 8.
9. Ibr Muqaffaʿ, *al-Adab al-saghir wa'l-adab al-kabir,* Beirut, 1960.
10. Cf. P. Cŕone, *Slaves on Horses,* and H.A.R. Gibb, *Studies on the Civilization of Islam*, op. cit.
11. See Malcolm Kerr, *Islamic Reform*, California, 1966, and P.J. Vatikiotis, *History of Egypt*, op. cit. on the controversy over the Caliphate and the Salafiyya movement of Sheikh Rashid Rida.
12. On this distinction, see the interesting book by M. Said Ashmawi, *Usul al-shariʿa*, Beirut, 1979, for which he was attacked by Radical and Militant Muslims.
13. Al-Ashmawi, op. cit. and Husein Ahmad Amin, *Hawla al-daʿwa ila tatbiq al-sharia.*
14. Abu al-Alla' al-Mawdudi, *The Political Theory of Islam*, Lahore, 1939, *The Islamic Way of Life*, Lahore, 1955, and *The Process of Islamic Revolution*, Lahore, 1955; and Muhammad Asad, *The Principles of State and Government in Islam*, Berkeley, California, 1961.
15. Gibb, *Modern Trends in Islam.*
16. Husein Ahmad Amin, *Hawla al-daʿwa ila tatbiq al-sharia*, and P.J. Vatikiotis, 'Authoritarianism and Autocracy', op. cit.
17. Gibb, *Modern Trends in Islam,* op. cit., p. 87.
18. Ibn Jamaa, *Tahrir al-ahkam fi tadbir ahl al-islam*, where he

restates the Sunni theory of the Caliphate soon after its destruction by the Mongols in 1258. Together with Ibn Taymiya, and depending on al-Ghazali's earlier work, op. cit., he accepts force or coercion as a necessary attribute of the Caliphate. This followed the earlier work of the traditional Muslim jurists, such as al-Mawardi, *Kitab al-ahkam al-sultaniyya*, op. cit. For a detailed discussion of these matters, see A.K.S. Lambton, op. cit., pp. 83–177.
19. Sura xxii (The Pilgrimage), esp. verse 78. (All Koranic suras and verses in English are from M. Pickthal, *The Glorious Koran*, 1954).

CHAPTER 2

1. Elie Kedourie, *Nationalism*, New York, 1960.
2. Ibid., and A.K.S. Lambton, op. cit.
3. Three vols., Cairo, 1898. See vol. 3 especially, pp. 60–5; also see edition edited by Ahmad Amin *et al.*, Cairo, 1952, vol. 3, pp. 222–5, 403–17.
4. For a survey of these developments, see A.K.S. Lambton, op. cit. and R. Levy, *The Social Structure of Islam*, Cambridge, 1957.
5. See Ibn al-Athir, *al-Kamil fi al-tarikh*, Bulaq, 1874 and Cairo, 1884–5; and Jahiz, *kitab al-mahasin wa'li-addad,* Leiden, 1898, and Cairo, 1906.
6. W.C. Smith, *Islam in Modern History*, Princeton, 1957.
7. Fazlur Rahman, *Islam*, London, 1966, especially pp. 212–34.
8. E. Kedourie, 'Concluding Remarks', in G.R. Warburg and U.M. Kuppeschmidt (eds.), *Islam, Nationalism and Radicalism in Egypt and the Sudan*, New York, 1983, pp. 385–402.
9. See some of the writings of Sayyid Qutb as cited elsewhere in the text and notes, and Abu al-Hasan al-Nadvi, op. cit.
10. V. Naipaul, *Among the Believers: An Islamic Journey*, London, 1981, pp. 99–209.
11. A. Laraoui, *The Crisis of the Arab Intellectual*, Berkeley, 1976. (Original French edition, Paris, 1974).
12. Roy P. Mottahedeh, *Loyalty and Leadership in Early Islamic Society*, Princeton, 1980.

CHAPTER 3

1. See on this relationship, among others, Hasan al-Ashmawi, *al-Ikhwan wa'l-thawra*, Cairo, 1977, Jabir Rizq, *Madhabih al-ikhwan fi sujun misr*, Cairo, 1977, and *Madhbahat al-ikhwan fi Liman Tura*. Also the memoirs of Mahmud Abd al-Halim, *al-Ikhwan al-muslimun: ahdath sana'at al-tarikh*, 2 vols., Alexandria, 1948.
2. See some of the writings by Hasan el-Banna and other leading Muslim Brothers cited in Chapter 5 below.
3. For a survey of some of these groups and organizations, see Saad el-Din Ibrahim, 'Anatomy of Egypt's Militant Islamic Groups: Methodological Note and Preliminary Findings', *International Journal*

of Middle Eastern Studies, vol. 12 (1980), 423–53, Olivier Carée and Gerard Michaud, *Les Frères Musulmans, Egypte et Syrie,* Paris, 1982, Gilles Kepel, *Muslim Extremism in Egypt: The Prophet and Pharoah*, California, 1986, Emmanuel Sivan, *Radical Islam: Medieval Theory and Modern Politics*, New Haven, 1985.

4. Sayyid Qutb, *Maalem fi'l-tariq*, Cairo and Beirut, 1964, *Fi zilal al-qur'an*, 5th edn., 8 vols., Beirut, 1967, and *al-ʿAdala al-ijtima ʿiya fi'l-islam*, Cairo, n.d.

5. *Al-kamil fi al-tarith* and *Mahasin wa'l-adad.*

6. Further on Nadvi, see Chapters 5 and 6, and for Qutb's notion of the sovereignty of God (*hakimiyyat Allah*) in his *Maalem fi'l-tariq,* op. cit.

7. See Ibn Taymiya, *al-Siyasa al-sharʿiyya,* op. cit.

8. E. Sivan, op. cit.

9. Abdel Qadir Auda, *al-Islam wa awdaʿuna al-siyasiya*, Cairo, 1978.

10. See Albert Hourani, *Arabic Thought in the Liberal Age*, London, 1962. One could argue that some of these liberal humanists were Christians.

11. See, for example, Khalid Muhammad Khalid, *Min huna nabda'*, Cairo, 1950, and Sadiq Jalal al-Azm, *Fi'l-naqd al-dhati*, Beirut, 1967, and *Naqd al-fikr al-dini*, Beirut, 1968.

12. E. Sivan, op. cit.

13. Ibid.

14. Sivan, ibid., refers to the findings of the Egyptian sociologist Sayyed Oweis, and those of the gynaecologist, Nawal al-Saʿdawi.

15. See P.J. Vatikiotis, 'Authoritarianism and Autocracy in the Middle East', op. cit.

16. W. Prescott, *History of the Reign of Ferdinand and Isabella, the Catholic, of Spain*, 3rd edn., London, 1841 (1st edn., 1838).

CHAPTER 4

1. It is interesting to note that in the famous Syrian Congress held in 1919 in Damascus in order to formulate, among other things, the Constitution of the first post-war independent Arab successor national state to the dissolved Muslim Ottoman Empire, under the monarchy of Amir Faysal of the Hejaz, delegates were divided over the issue of the separation between religion and politics, religion and state. One group, the 'progressive modernists', comprising those Syrians educated in modern secular letters and the law, argued that the Arab Syrian nation looked forward to the dawn of a new era dominated by the objective of establishing a state that complied with the spirit of the age, that is, one in which religion had no place. Divine religions, they argued further, should confine themselves to performing their holy tasks, while politics evolved according to the needs of the national interest, just as in the case of the advanced nations in Europe and America. Separating politics from religion did not mean the neglect of religion, or ignoring its high ideals and edifying values as truth,

humanity and brotherly love; it meant only that religious belief cannot dictate state policy which is clearly liable to change from time to time, whereas religious belief is permanent and immutable. Moreover, the nation comprises citizens of different religions. '[We] The Syrians could not continue in a situation when history has clearly shown the shortcomings of the involvement of religion in politics. It creates serious differences among the citizens and sectarian fragmentation in the body politic. It is therefore preferable to allow religion to retain its sacred and inimitable character and politics its very mundane territorial feature which is liable to change from the pressures of the environment and circumstances. This way religion and politics can each follow its respective separate course in the same community.' (See Yousef al-Hakim, *Suriyya wa'l 'ahd al-faysali* (Syria in Feisal's Era), Beirut, 1966, pp. 96–7.)

2. P.J. Vatikiotis, *Conflict in the Middle East*, London, 1971, p. 199.

3. Anonymous review in the *TLS*, December 1971, and ensuing furore. The episode was fully discussed by J.B. Kelly, 'The *TLS* in the Desert', in the *Journal of Commonwealth History*, vol. 1. Incidentally, the episode ended the era of anonymous reviews in the *TLS*, and coincidentally perhaps a new editor took over the *TLS* soon thereafter. The episode also elicited attacks in the national press on anonymous reviewing for the *TLS* by Frank Kermode and Hugh Trevor-Roper, as he was then.

4. See A.K.S. Lambton, op. cit., and W.C. Smith, op. cit.

5. H.A. Amin, *Hawla'l-da'wa ila tatbiq al-sharīʿa*, pp. 89–100.

6. See M. Said Ashmawi, *Usul al-sharīʿa*, op. cit.

7. Recently, Muslims have focused their propaganda efforts (especially in Western Europe) against secularism and for the advancement of Islam's view of and presence in the world: both measures directed at the objective of restoring world power to Islam. Thus they attribute secularism in the West to the West's reaction against the behaviour of the medieval Church, denying in this way the notion that secularism is underpinned by any particular scale of values, or ethic regarding man, nature, society and morality. This approach is perhaps a reflection of ignorance and arrogance. Then the Saudi-financed newspaper, *al-Sharq al-awsat*, published in London, carries a 'religion and heritage' page on which it discusses Islam and technology, *sharia* or Islamic law, trade and commerce, financial and banking institutions. It usually consists of a mindless mixture, or hotch-potch, of assertion, excuse and self-justification for any shortcomings, but rarely cogent and coherent analytical argument. Instances of this hazardous activity are the cases of Judge Ashmawi and Ambassador Husein Ahmad Amin. They were both violently and consistently attacked by the publications of the Muslim Brethren and the militant Radical Muslim organizations, as well as by the official Azharite religious establishment. Judge Ashmawi resorted for redress to the national civil courts. In the meantime, the state had to provide him with physical protection against possible molestation by militants. Ambassador Husein Amin had to be posted abroad and as far away from his critics and detractors as possible. He is currently in Brazil. The Copt literary critic, essayist and cultural

historian, Dr Louis Awad, a prominent and consistent secularist for forty years, also came under the sharp and sustained attack of the official religious establishment as well as that of the radicals.

8. See Baghdadi's classic, *al-Farq bayna'l-firaq*, Cairo, 1910, and Shahrastani's equally classic, *Kitab al-milal wa'l-nihal fi'l-islam*, 2 parts in one, Bulaq, 1874 and Cairo, 1951.

9. See *Madha Khasira'l-ʿalam binhitat al-muslimin* (What the World has Lost by the Decline of the Muslims), 8th printing, Kuwait, 1980. In discussing the Ottomans, Nadvi laments the loss of their leadership, and their state as the shield of Islam against an advanced and advancing Europe. In it Nadvi recalls, the Ottoman state had a huge navy and controlled 800,000 square miles of territory from the Caucasus to the Atlas Mountains in the west, and from Africa in the south to the Danube in the north. Within that area Islam held sway materially and spiritually. (See pp. 159–70.) Despite its decline and the corruption of its rulers before its destruction, the Ottoman state was none the less a formidable fortress of Islam and a wide, powerful wall — obstacle — which protected the Muslim Arab provinces including Palestine and the Hejaz, from the interference of Western foreign powers. This was the situation up until the Sultanate of Abdel Hamid (deposed 1909) who, despite all that has been said of him, prevented every Christian attempt and every Jewish conspiracy against the Muslim holy places (i.e. Mecca, Medina and Jerusalem) until the Great War, when the Allies succeeded in attracting the Arabs to their side, thus separating the Arab provinces from the Ottoman empire, and recasting them as nation-states which, even when they attained independence, had no strong hand to protect them. Israel, herself a creation of big European powers, was eventually able to dominate these new states and to possess holy Jerusalem for the first [*sic.*] time in history. 'The end of the Ottoman Empire in the east', he laments, 'was the greatest victory for crusader Europe and world Judaism'.

10. Beirut, 1981.

CHAPTER 5

1. A slightly different text of this chapter will appear in M. Esman and I. Rabinovitch *Ethnicity, Pluralism and Conflict in the Middle East.* Ithaca, N.Y., 1987.

2. Y. al-Qardawi, *Ghayr al-muslimin fi'l-mujtama 'al-islami*, Alexandria 1977.

3. For example, Y. al-Qardawi, *al-Halal wa'l-haram fi'l-islam* (11 printings); *al-Hall al-islami, farida wa durura* (2 printings); *al-Iman wa'l-hayat* (5 editions).

4. G. Badawi, *al-Fitna al-ta'ifiyya fi misr: judhuruha wa asbabuha*, Cairo, 1977.

5. W. Suleiman, *al-Hiwar bayna'l-adyan*, Cairo, 1976.

6. Cairo, 1980.

7. M. al-Bahiy, *al-Fikr al-islami wa'l-mujtama' 'al-mu'asir: mushkilat al-hukm wa'l-tawjih,* Cairo, 1965 (2nd edn, 1975, 3rd edn, 1983). See also the companion volume, *Mushkilat al-usra wa al-takaful*, Cairo, 1967 (3rd edition, 1982).

8. M.S. Zaki, *al-Ikhwan al-muslimun wa'l-mujtama al-misri*, second impression, Cairo, 1980.

9. M. Hanna, *Aqbat na'am . . . wa lakinna misriyyin*, Cairo, 1980.

10. See A.H. Metwalli, *Azamat al-fikr al-siyasi al-islami,* Alexandria, 1970. See also several works on administrative and constitutional law (1936–52), and his later *Masadir al-ahkam al-dusturiyya fi'l-shari'a al-islamiyya*, Cairo, 1963; 'Al-islam wa mushkilat al-siyada fi'l-dawla', *Majallat al-huquq*, nos. 1 and 2, 1964–65; 'Mabadi' nizam al-hukm fi'l-islam', and 'Al-islam wa hal huwa din wa dawla', in *Majallat al-qanun wa'l-iqtisad*, Cairo University, no. 4, 1964, and no. 5, 1965.

11. For example, Y. al-Qardawi: 'Society that has accepted Islam as the basis of its life and conduct, a constitution for its government and a source for its legislation and the direction (instruction and guidance) for all matters of life, individual and social, material and moral, local and international', op. cit., p. 5. Abdel Qadir Auda: 'Islamic rule is the best the world has known' *(al-Islam wa awda 'una al-siyasiyya*, Cairo, 1978, p. 8). He refers to Sura iii:85, 'And who so seeketh as religion other than the Surrender [to Allah: i.e. Islam] it will not be accepted from him, and he will be a loser in the Hereafter'. (All Koranic suras and verses in English are from M. Pickthal, *The Glorious Koran*, New York, 1954). According to Auda the Muslim has no choice because, 'And becometh not a believing man or a believing woman when Allah and His Messenger have decided an affair [for them], that they should [after that] claim any say in their affair; and who so is rebellious to Allah and His Messenger, he verily goeth astray in error manifest' (Sura xxxiii:36). Moreover, all these writers depend on the revelation, 'Who so judgeth not by that which Allah hath revealed: such are disbelievers' (Sura v:44), repeated in verse 47. Sayyid Qutb, too, in asserting that Islamic society is the only one in which faith is the bond of political association (*Ma'alem fi'l-tariq*, op. cit., p. 146), refers repeatedly to these revelations: 'So judge between them by that which Allah hath revealed . . .' (Sura v:49); 'Ye are the best community that hath been raised up for mankind . . . And if the People of the Scripture had believed it had been better for them. Some of them are believers; but most of them are evil-livers' (Sura iii:110).

12. Vol. 1, parts 1 and 2, London, 1950 and 1957.

13. A.S. Tritton, *Non-Muslim Subjects of Muslim Rulers*, Cambridge, 1930, pp. 229, 230–1, and 232; Arabic translation Ali Husni al-Kharbutli, *al-Islam wa ahl al-dhimma*, Cairo, n.d.; and Abd al-Karim Zaydan, *Ahkam al-dhimmiyyin wa'l-musta'minin fi dar al-Islam*, Cairo, n.d.

14. London, 1947.

15. Ibid., p. 22.

16. It should be noted that the communal trouble in Khanka in Egypt in 1972 involved the use of the premises of a Coptic lay society

for church services, without a permit from the Ministry of the Interior. See Gamal Badawi, *al-Fitna al-ta'ifiyya fi misr*, op. cit.

17. Sura ix:29: 'Fight against such of those who have been given the Scripture as believe not in Allah nor in the Last Day, and forbid not that which Allah hath forbidden by His Messenger, and follow now the religion of truth until they pay the tribute readily, *being brought low*'. (Italics added.)

18. Syria, Iraq, Iran, even Egypt. The official religion of the state in all of these is Islam. Neither radical nationalism and socialism led by Egypt in the 1950s and 1960s, nor Baathism in the Fertile Crescent, succeeded in separating religion from the state. See P.J. Vatikiotis, 'Authoritarianism and Autocracy in the Middle East', op. cit., pp. 135–51.

19. See P.J. Vatikiotis, 'The Crisis in Lebanon: a local historical perspective', *The World Today*, March 1984, pp. 85–92, esp. p. 92.

20. In A.L. Udovitch (ed.), *The Middle East: Oil, Conflict and Hope*, Lexington, Mass., 1976, pp. 181–94.

21. A perusal of the writings of the Muslim Brethren until today is clear and ample evidence of this requirement. See especially, Hasan al-Banna, *Majmu'at rasa'il*, Cairo, n.d.; Abdel Qadir Auda, op. cit.; Sayyid Qutb, *Nahwa mujtama' islami*, Amman, 1969, and *Ma'alem fi'l-tariq*, op. cit.

22. Ibid.

23. Suras lxiv:8, iv:141, viii:7, and 39.

24. Hasan al-Banna, *Majmu'at rasa'il*, op. cit., p. 19.

25. Ibid., p. 20 and pp. 180–4.

26. He uses sura ix:32: 'Fain would they put out the light of Allah with their mouths, but Allah disdaineth [aught] save that He shall perfect his light, however much the disbelievers are averse'.

27. Sayyid Qutb, *Ma'alem* op. cit., is particularly adamant on this point. And so are all the other Muslim Brothers. See especially Zaynab al-Ghazali, *Ayyam min hayati*, Cairo and Beirut, 1982.

28. Qardawi, op. cit., p. 20.

29. Ibid., p. 82.

30. Ibid., p. 82.

31. Ibid., p. 83.

32. See especially Qutb, *Ma'alim*, op. cit., and Abdel Qadir Auda, op. cit.

33. Note the adamance of Zaynab al-Ghazali, op. cit., who repeatedly appeals to sura iii:28: 'Let not the believers take disbelievers for their friends in preference to believers. Who so doeth he hath no connection with Allah unless [it be] that ye but guard yourselves against them, taking [as it were] security. Allah biddeth you beware [only] of Himself. Unto Allah is the journeying'.

34. Ahmad al-Bahiy, *al-Fikr al-islami*, op. cit., 1982 edition, p. 371.

35. A.H. Metwalli, *Azamat al-Fikr*, op. cit.

36. Sura iii:19: 'Lo! religion with Allah [is] the Surrender . . .'

37. Sura iii:85: 'And who so seeketh as religion other than the Surrender [to Allah] it will not be accepted from him, and he will be a loser in the Hereafter'.

38. Abdel Qadir Auda, op. cit., using sura xxxi:13: '. . . Ascribe no partners unto Allah. Lo! to ascribe partners [unto Him] is a tremendous wrong'; and sura ii:254: '. . . The disbelievers, they are the wrongdoers'. See also S. Qutb, *Ma'alem*, op. cit., pp. 200–2.

39. See Abdel Qadir Auda, op. cit., p. 65. See also Abu al-Hasan al-Nadvi, *Madha Khasira al-'alam*, op. cit.

40. Ibid., pp. 70–5.

41. On Judaism and the Jews especially, see Ali Husni al-Kharbutli, *al-Arab wa'l-yahud fi'l-'asr al-islami,* Cairo, n.d.; and *al-'Ilaqat al-siyasiyya bayna'l-arab wa'l-yahud*, Cairo, 1969.

42. Qutb, *Nahwa mujtama' islami*, op. cit., p. 53.

43. Ibid., pp. 110, 130.

44. Ibid., pp. 87–131, and *Ma'alem*, op. cit., pp. 86–9.

45. Qutb, *Nahwa mujtama' islami*, op. cit., pp. 184–5.

46. Qutb, *Ma'alem*, op. cit., pp. 192–3, 198.

47. Ibid., pp. 200–2.

48. Ibid., pp. 202–8.

49. See Zaynab al-Ghazali, op. cit.

50. Here I refer to developments in these countries at least since the 1930s.

51. See Gamal Badawi, op. cit., for details, esp. pp. 9–17.

52. See Milad Hanna, op. cit., Zaynab al-Ghazali, op. cit., and Ahmad al-Bahiy, op. cit.

53. See the interesting argument by Tariq al-Bishri, *al-muslimun wa'l-agbat fi itar al-jama'a al-wataniyya*, Cairo, 1980, pp. 679–750.

54. Ibid., and Abdel Qadir Auda, op. cit., pp. 90–2.

55. Recently a copy of 'A Model of an Islamic Constitution' was sent to me by The Secretary-General of the Islamic Council. Two of the suras introducing the publication are iv:105: 'We have revealed to you the Book with the truth so that you may judge between people by that which Allah has shown you; so do not plead for the treacherous', and sura v:44: 'Those who do not judge in accordance with what Allah has revealed are the unbelievers'. The Introduction is interesting:

> The contemporary Islamic world is passing through a period of creative tension; 'tension' because the real state of affairs, at individual, collective and state levels, is generally at variance with the ideals and norms of Islam; 'creative' because this tension has released forces positive and powerful enough to bring about an upsurge in the Muslim world directed towards making Islam the guiding light in the reconstruction of individual and social life . . .'

It also records the Muslims' 'disillusionment with secular ideologies and their firm resolve to build their society on the foundations of Islam':

> The Qur'an has enunciated not only moral norms for the individual, and rules and regulations for family and social life, but also a number of civil, commercial criminal, constitutional and international laws and principles of judicial conduct. Unless there is an

> Islamic state, parts of the Shari'ah will remain in suspension.

Article 14, Chapter 2, 'Obligations and Rights', reads: '(b) Every Muslim has a right to seek citizenship of the State . . .'

There is no explicit statement regarding citizenship for non-Muslims. Article 16, regarding non-Muslims, para (c) reads:

> In matters of personal law the minorities shall be governed by their own laws and traditions, except if they themselves opt to be governed by the Shari'ah. In case of conflict between parties, the Shari'ah shall apply.

Article 18(a) states:

> Citizens have a right to assemble and to form groups, scientific, social and other — as long as their programmes and activities are consistent with the provisions of the Shari'ah.

Finally, Articles 24 and 26 suggest that non-Muslims are disqualified from holding elected office.

CHAPTER 6

1. P.J. Vatikiotis, 'Terrorism in the Lands of Islam', in Benjamin Netanyahu (ed.), *International Terrorism: How the West can Win*, New York, 1985, pp. 77–83.

Index

For Product Safety Concerns and Information please contact our EU
representative GPSR@taylorandfrancis.com
Taylor & Francis Verlag GmbH, Kaufingerstraße 24, 80331 München, Germany

www.ingramcontent.com/pod-product-compliance
Lightning Source LLC
Chambersburg PA
CBHW050531270326
41926CB00015B/3172

* 9 7 8 1 1 3 8 2 1 9 8 4 7 *